CHAUTAUQUA IMPRESSIONS

ARCHITECTURE AND AMBIENCE

Fount before Post Office, by Fred Torrey.

ART

Fountain, center-piece of Bestor Plaza - sculptural
element by Fred Torrey of Chicago

Richard N. Campen
Photographs by the author

CHAUTAUQUA IMPRESSIONS

ARCHITECTURE AND AMBIENCE

Fourth Printing – Available from Selden W. Campen
20670 University Blvd., Shaker Heights, OH 44122 • (216) 932-1555

Dedicated to my sons -
Richard Selden Campen
and
Selden William Campen

The "**Chautauqua Belle**"

BOOKS BY RICHARD N. CAMPEN

GEORGE BROWN OF GATES MILLS

ARCHITECTURE OF THE WESTERN RESERVE: 1800 - 1900

OHIO — AN ARCHITECTURAL PORTRAIT

OUR VALLEY . . . OUR VILLAGES —
   AN ILLUSTRATED STORY OF THE CHAGRIN VALLEY

GERMAN VILLAGE PORTRAIT (Columbus, Ohio)

SANIBEL AND CAPTIVA . . . ENCHANTING ISLANDS

OUTDOOR SCULPTURE IN OHIO

(all illustrated with photographs by the author)

DESIGN BY RICHARD N. CAMPEN

Copyright ©1984, 1997 Selden W. Campen
Library of Congress Catalog Card Number 83-051428
All rights reserved
ISBN 0-9601356-3-4
Type-face - Paladium
Paper - Productolith
Printed in the United States of America

Cover - 'TIONESTA' a water color by Christine Vaughn
Back Cover - Calligraphy by Jackie Briggs, Jamestown, N.Y.

The "Sea Lion"

CONTENTS

COLOR PLATE INDEX

Page 17
Top - **Bestor Plaza**, Colonnade Building, Fountain sculpture by Fred Torrey.
Bottom - **Miller Bell Tower** at Fair Point.

Page 35
Top left - **The Hall of Philosophy** (1903- 1906), Albert Kelsey, architect. A Greek Temple without cella.
Top right - **Genevieve Cheney Cottage** (1899), #18 Cookman. Viewed from the Hall of Philosophy.
Bottom left - **Autumn** - all quiet at the Amphitheatre and Screen House.
Bottom right - **Smith Library** (1931) - rear aspect from 'Amphitheatre Plaza'.

Page 53
Top left - **The Brick Walk** south from the Amphitheatre.
Top right - **Chapel of the Good Shepherd** (c. 1895)
Bottom left - **Norton Memorial Hall** (1929), Otis Floyd Johnson/Lorado Taft, architects.
Bottom right - **The Hall of Christ** (1900-1909) Paul J. Peltz, arch't.

Page 71
Top left - **Hurlbut Church** (1931) Pratt Avenue.
Top right - **Bestor Plaza** viewed from Smith Library.
Bottom left - **The Athenaeum Hotel** (1881) South Lake Drive.
Bottom right - **Plaza before Amphitheatre**, United Methodist House viewed from Smith Library.

Page 89
Top left - **Chautauqua Post Office** (1909), Bestor Plaza - Book Store entrance at left.
Top right - **Welch's Pavilion**, Fountain 'house' - southeast corner of Bestor Plaza.
Bottom left - **Morning lecture** at the Amphitheatre.
Bottom right - **The Chautauqua Inn** (c. 1876) 16 North Terrace Ave.

Page 107
Top left - **Baird-Wineman Cottage** (c. 1895), #5 Peck Avenue - a riot of color!
Top right - **"Box Seat"** (1888), 30 Clark Avenue.
Bottom - **The Walter McIntosh Cottage** (1883), #12 Bowman Avenue.

Page 125
Top left - **The Miller Bell Tower** (1911) - symbol of Chautauqua.
Top right - **"The Aldine"** apartments, Bowman Avenue at Simpson.
Bottom - **The Compton-Freytag Cottage** (1914-16), corner of Pratt and Hurst. An oriental touch.

Opposite Page 127
Top left - **The Taylor Cottage** (1881), 38 Miller.
Top right - **Willard-Haller Cottage** (1883), 32 South Lake Drive. - one of Chautauqua's most picturesque.
Bottom left - **Lake Chautauqua** viewed from "College Hill".
Bottom right - **United Methodist Missionary Home** (1903), 34 South Lake Drive - noteworthy for its marvelous Arts and Crafts interior.

Fig. 3 **The "Aldine"**, a rooming house at #20 Simpson, corner of Bowman.

FOREWORD

A number of years ago an architect friend, well aware of my writings about Ohio's landmark architecture, suggested that I turn my attention to Chautauqua. In the intervening years other writing projects vied more successfully for my time. However, in the late 1960's, when returning from a summer of camping and research in Maine, my wife and I had detoured to Chautauqua as the season was winding-up. I recall seeing the famed amphitheatre, but not much else. We were traveling in a small Shasta trailer; no one seemed to know of a campground in the vicinity (indeed there was none) so we arranged to park our vehicle at the service station which then occupied the corner - north of the Institution where NY-430 joins NY-394 - and where, at least, we had a rest-room at our disposal. This need has been mightily rectified in the intervening years.

The same friend, upon another occasion when I made inquiry about a quiet place, not too far from Cleveland, to spend New Year's eve, suggested the St. Elmo Hotel at Chautauqua as a possible alternative. We did, this time, heed his advice. The lobby, that late December, was very cozy, the food good and nicely served, our quarters adequate. It was one of those bleak, overcast, year-end holiday week-ends typical of this lower Great Lakes region. At that time many older ladies stayed the winter at the St. Elmo. In the company of friends, we were not the least disappointed at the quietness of Chautauqua. Once again, however, I failed to react to the environment; I do not even recall seeing Norton Hall or the Hall of Philosophy. As I now look back, this seems exceedingly strange.

In the summer of 1982 our youngest son, looking for a place to camp and to sail, "found" Lake Chautauqua and the Chautauqua Institution. We recall that he was particularly impressed with Betty Bao Lord, author of **Spring Moon** - a volume which he and we read forthwith. Returning to Cleveland he said to me, "Dad, you would be wild about Chautauqua; it is just your cup-of-tea." He was so enthusiastic that he had rented quarters for his family for the entire 1983 season. In the spring he shared the advance season program with us. Thus encouraged and stimulated, we knew that we would spend time at Chautauqua during the summer of '83.

We have another older son and grand-children in New York City whom, by June of 1983, we had not seen since the previous December - the intervening months having been passed at our Sanibel island beach-house. We planned to drive to New York to see them in June. With the prospect of spending some part of the summer at Chautauqua, I recalled the erstwhile suggestion of my architect friend that I take-a-look at Chautauqua. Maybe - just maybe - Chautauqua's architecture would be of interest to me as a book project. With this thought in mind I dispatched a letter to Dr. Robert Hesse, President, advising of my potential interest and of my intention to stop by en route to New York. Additionally, I wished to investigate what books had been done to date and to see if I could "warm-up" to Chautauqua.

In Chautauqua I was referred to Mr. Phil Zimmer, Director of Communications who immediately expressed interest in what I might do book-wise (I had dispatched a couple of my previous volumes as a precursor of my personal visit). He offered full cooperation. For the balance of the day my wife and I roamed about the grounds as I enthusiastically exposed a roll of film. Chautauqua was fresh and green; one sensed the anticipation of the coming season in all the painting and preparation in progress. Older, wiser and under these ideal conditions, I was totally captivated by all that I saw. The Hall of Philosophy, on which I laid my eyes for the first time, particularly impressed me; I had something of the feeling of being on a college campus. In the Book Store I was invited to sit down and browse through Alfreda Irwin's **Three Taps of the Gavel** and Pauline Fancher's **Chautauqua: Its Architecture and Its People.** Could I do anything different or better? Both have much merit. I was not convinced when we departed Chautauqua and for several days thereafter.

However, before too long I persuaded myself that with my background in architectural history, enhanced by travels over much of this earth with architecture as the focus, and with my photographic abilities, I might be able to do a book more selective in the choice of its architectural images, more interesting for its critical observations and perhaps more spontaneous. I would endeavor to make it a beautiful book in which not only I could take pride, but also the Institution itself and the legions of those who love Chautauqua, as well. At this point I made a commitment to the project and so advised Mssrs. Hesse and Zimmer mindful of a printed piece on "Commitment" posted in this studio which I would like to share with my reader, as follows:

> Until one is committed there is hesitancy, the chance to draw back, always ineffectiveness. Concerning all acts of iniative (and creation), there is one elementary truth, the ignorance of which kills countless ideas and splendid plans: that the moment one definitely commits oneself, then Providence moves too. All sorts of things occur to help one that would never otherwise have occurred. A whole stream of events issues from the decision, raising in one's favor all manner of unforseen incidents . . . which no man could have dreamt would come his way. I have learned at deep respect for one of Goethe's couplets: "Whatever you can do or dream you can do, begin it. Boldness has genius, power and magic in it."

I own a debt of gratitude to both Pauline Fancher and Alfreda Irwin, true historians, who spent countless hours scouring ancient **Assembly Heralds** and **Chautauqua Dailys** for information; also to Theodore Morrison for his fine **Chautauqua: A Center for Education, Religion and Artists in America** and to the sixty-odd persons, under Ms. Fancher's supervision, who canvassed every cottage on the grounds for

Fig. 4 **The Arcade** - alternate close-up aspect. cf. also Fig. 101 page 77.

information concerning ownership, building dates, etc. which enabled Chautauqua to qualify as a New York State Historic Site in 1973. I have not hesitated to use the dates and other information gleaned from this research. Little is to be gained by repeating the spade-work of others; better to build from that base. I also wish to express appreciation to Ms. Barbara Haug, in charge of the History Desk at Smith Library, to Mrs. William Leonard of the History section, and to Mr. and Mrs. Edgar Shields of Chagrin Falls, Ohio, for making their cottage at #12 Bliss Avenue available to me.

In conclusion, while much history may be gleaned from the book in hand, it does not pretend to be a history of Chautauqua. It is, rather, an appreciation, a selective, singling-out of its worthy architecture with critical comment and it is impressions - in word and picture.

Richard N. Campen
January 1984

Fig. 5 **Christine Vaughn** - 1983 Bell Tower scholar - painting in Miller Park. The cover art is hers.

INTRODUCTION

Impressions from Overseas

I was privileged to win an English Speaking Union/Chautauqua Scholarship and for six weeks during the summer of 1983 found myself living and working in this wonderland. Little did I realize what was in store for me. In England the only reference to Chautauqua I found was in a guide book where it was described as being situated on a lake and that it was a good place for sailing. Mention was also made of a summer school. These are certainly aspects, but I feel that they give an inadequate picture. It is a cliché to say that Chautauqua is very difficult to describe. Facets can be enumerated, but these cannot fully describe the essence of the place. It has to be **experienced** and I was fortunate enough to be able to do so.

I vividly remember the initial impact: the strongest first impression it made on me was the peace, the tranquility, the quality of relaxation. As a teacher coming from the hectic end-of-term buzz and the frenetic pace of New York City - weary with traveling, time changes and culture shock, Chautauqua seemed an idyllic haven. Its sheer natural beauty was outstanding and inspiring. I was soon to find, also, the kindliness, friendliness and generosity of the people I met there.

As a practicing artist and teacher of Art and the History of Art I found Chautauqua amazingly rich. It was mainly in the areas of painting and photography that I worked, using the natural surroundings as the major subject matter. Architecture is the chief interest in my work and Chautauqua was inspirational. I felt that I had an insight into a piece of America which had remained unaltered or unspoiled since the Victorian era. Here was a wealth of structures made of wood, displaying verandahs and porches, irregular gables, shuttered windows, intricate wooden tracery, asymmetrical staircases - all in a myriad of colors juxtaposed one against the other, set against leafy magnificent trees and the lake.

This environment of incredible serenity and perfect beauty is conducive to creativity and, indeed, nurtures it. I had the opportunity to work here, to enjoy the facilities offered by the Art School and to benefit from the exchange of ideas with the instructors and fellow students of outstanding talent. It was an exciting environment in which to work. To a foreigner Chautauqua seems a part of America unchanged and timeless - upholding many American ideals. In some respects it appears divorced from reality, but it generates its own richness and exists in its own timelessness. I know that the memory of the six weeks which I spent at Chautauqua will remain with me for the rest of my life.

Christine Vaughn
Bell Tower Scholar 1983
Barnet, Hertfordshire, England

Fig. 6 **The Landon Cottage** (1876) - Miller Park at Whitfield - although built by W. M. Mossman, the house takes the name of grandson, Alfred Landon, 1936 nominee of the Republican Party.

Fig. 7 **CLSC Headquarters** on the Brick Walk opposite Smith Library

FIRST IMPRESSIONS

For the past month and more I have been deeply immersed in the multiple facets of life at Chautauqua Institution during its one hundred and ninth summer session. Only one familiar with Chautauqua's varied offerings can fully comprehend how busy it is possible to be: with morning lectures by authorities in such diverse subjects as science, economics, literary criticism and the arts, with brown-bag luncheon demonstrations at the Arts and Crafts Center, with afternoon programs on moral and religious issues followed by illustrated lectures sponsored by the Bird, Tree and Garden Club, travel films, nature walks . . . and finally, with evening programs by either the Chautauqua Symphony or Chautauqua Festival orchestras (the latter a superb ensemble of serious music students - most of whom attend the nation's leading graduate and undergraduate schools of music) . . . all augmented with periodic performances by The Opera Company, the Acting Company and the Dance Department. Indeed, Chautauqua is a "culture vultures" delight!

Moreover, within the past few days I have attended the traditional, ceremonial rites of Old First Night and CLSC Recognition Day. In earlier times, a century ago, each summer 'Assembly' was initiated by a "first night" service which is literally repeated to this day, but rather at mid-term, in early August, since the summer session is now so much longer. Today, moreover, the traditional service is augmented with lively presentations by each of the performing arts groups in residence, thereby, introducing music, theatre and dance to this festive evening at the conclusion of which every one of the several thousand persons in attendance receives a piece of an eight-hundred pound birthday cake. CLSC Recognition Day, which follows, requires a bit more explaining. Suffice it to say, at this point, that on this most important day on the Chautauqua calendar, participants in the Chautauqua Learning and Science Circle program who have met the prescribed reading requirements over a period of four years receive their diplomas (recognition) and become honored members of what might be thought of as an august, inner circle of Chautauquans.

As I experienced these programs which bare the heart and soul of Chautauqua, I commenced to speculate on why this Institution has persisted and continues strong and vital after well over a century while so many others have fallen by the wayside. This is a long time in the course of human affairs; the map of the world has been remade over these epochal decades. A great deal of dedication and treasure is required to carry on Chautauqua's diverse activities, its lecture series, its scholarships in music, in art and in dance. This enduring and noble experiment could conceivably have lost its momentum following a decade of faltering management, but it has not and, in fact, today appears healthier than ever if one may judge by the ever-increasing attendance, the loyalty of families who have been returning for up to seven generations and the laudatory remarks one hears from every quarter. Indeed, there is a renaissance taking place at Chautauqua.

Why then, I asked myself, does Chautauqua survive and thrive? There is certainly more than one answer, but surely its adaptability to changing times and circumstances figures importantly; living things adapt or they die! The answer is also to be found in that Chautauqua offers something in abundance for everybody . . .: intellectual stimulation, spiritual solice, instruction in many arts and crafts, a summer camping experience for children and family recreation in its beautiful, wooded preserve on the shores of scenic Lake Chautauqua.

Furthermore, Chautauqua offers a unique experience. Where else in America can one partake of so diverse a bill-of-cultural fare? Where else can the serious high school and/or collegiate musician study his instrument, play in a superbly rehearsed orchestra and, at the same time, listen to and learn from, the tri-weekly performances of a professional, symphonic orchestra? Chautauqua's uniqueness is also to be found in its marvelous ambience—particularly the many quaint cottages from Victorian times which are a principal focus of this volume; cottages which have survived in this sylvan retreat—not here threatened by the rampant expansion, neglect and misuse which has swept away such valuable and picturesque period-pieces in our cities. From an architectural and environmental perspective, in large degree, to visit Chautauqua is to turn the clock back to Victorian times. Here-in lies its charm!

A number of years ago at mid-morning in the course of touring Austria, perhaps at Bad Ischl, the beautiful strains of a Viennese waltz reached my ears. I stopped and headed towards its source - a well fenestrated pavilion. I recall photographing a bust of Franz Lehar located in a garden setting nearby. Within this pavilion a string orchestra was playing the lilting music of Strauss, Lanner, Lehar and others so reminiscent of the gay, carefree Vienna of Franz Josef early in this century. It was peopled by couples partaking of the local mineral water—seated, relaxed, listening. It was beautiful! - the music, the scene; I had never experienced such a dignified, civilized passing of time before. I joined it briefly before proceeding eastward to Florian, Steyr and Vienna.

This summer Chautauqua kept reminding me of that memorable, serendipitous, Austrian encounter as mornings in the venerable amphitheatre, I joined hundreds of others in listening to the speaker of the day, likewise afternoons, in the wonderful, open-air Hall of Philosophy, or, again, at the Amphitheatre where, when not in use for a scheduled program, one may listen to a rehearsal by one of the resident orchestras while catching-up on the daily news, reading a book, or engaging in needle-work. Chautauqua, too, I discovered, is a most civilized place.

Fig. 8 **Music student practices** his bass viol near McKnight Hall.

Fig. 9 **Fair Point**, Miller Bell Tower and College Club - point of landing for the thousands who came to Chautauqua by boat for over fifty years from 1874.

HISTORICAL SKETCH

The work in hand is not intended to be a history of Chautauqua; its history has been recorded by others, to whom I am indebted, steeped in much greater degree, in the lore of Chautauqua, (cf. bibliography). However, it seems desirable for those persons for whom this book may be the introduction to the Institution to, in barest outline, review its history.

Chautauqua was the dream of Lewis Miller of Akron, Ohio, who was born (at nearby Greentown) on the 24th of July in the year 1829. At that very time the old Ohio Canal, connecting the lake port of Cleveland with Portsmouth on the Ohio River, was being pushed through Akron - the highest point in this ambitious project. The canal opened markets for Ohio's produce in the East, via Lake Erie and New York's just completed Erie Canal, and in the South, via the Ohio and Mississippi Rivers. Cleveland's population at this time was 1,075; Akron's a few hundred. By age sixteen Lewis Miller was a school teacher; at age twenty he worked as a plasterer having entered the world of business by age seventeen. Obviously a person of ambition and quality, he plied his trade in the summer and studied in the winter. In due course he apprenticed himself in a machine shop, eventually becoming foreman, then superintendent and finally proprietor of his own business engaged in manufacturing farm implements including the well-regarded Buckeye Mower and Reaper which he invented. The success of this business enabled him to live well and to turn his energies in other philanthropic directions. Aside from business, he became keenly interested in Sunday school work; he organized a normal school to train young people to teach in his school and designed an advanced plan for Sunday schools which won considerable acceptance. His interest in education and public service is further illustrated in that for years he served on the Akron Board of Education and was a life trustee of Mount Union College in Alliance, Ohio. During these years he lived comfortably with his family in a lovely home in the Oak Park section of Akron.

In the very early 1870's Miller dreamed of a secluded, summer assembly for the up-grading of Sunday school instruction. At this very time he came in contact with John Heyl Vincent, secretary of Sunday school work for the Methodist denomination, who was born in Tuscaloosa, Alabama in 1832. When Vincent was six years of age his family moved to Pennsylvania where he received his education at Milton and Lewisburg Academies; later he attended Weslyan Institute in Newark, New Jersey. By age seventeen he was licensed to preach and preach he did, traveling by horseback in circuits, between 1851 and 1865. In the latter year he founded a Sunday School quarterly while based in Chicago. His lesson systems were adopted internationally. Commencing in 1868 he served as Sunday School agent and Secretary of the Methodist Episcopal Church. It was in this capacity that he came in contact with Lewis Miller.

Obviously the two men's interests, experience and vision complemented one another. We have seen that as a Methodist Sunday School Superintendent in Akron, Miller had organized a normal class to train young people to teach in his school - that he dreamed of a summer assembly to carry on this work in a removed, out-of-doors situation. To this end he enlisted Vincent as superintendent and co-founder of what was to become the Chautauqua Assembly which then held its first session, attended by over 500 select students, for two weeks in August, 1874, at Fair Point - site of a recently established Chautauqua Lake Camp Meeting Reservation. These grounds, ultimately consisting of several hundred acres bordering the Lake, were within a few years deeded to Miller and Vincent's Chautauqua Assembly. While initially the term of the Assembly was but two weeks, this time-frame gradually increased to a month, then forty days until today, as the Chautauqua Institution, with somewhat changed objective and focus, the "season" lasts for approximately two months.

The Chautauqua ideal is as valid today as when articulated by founder Lewis Miller in the excerpt which follows from the speech made by him on First Night in 1888:

"We are all one on these grounds. No matter to what denomination you belong; no matter what creed, no matter to what political party of the country. You are welcome here whether high or low. You have a right to go anywhere you can get . . . here you are welcome to go about examining the various organizations and the various schemes and methods that are brought forward . . . and introduced to you, taking such thing as you want. Believe just what you want to (believe) and what you please (to believe) about them and take them with you or leave them here as you please. And you are entirely welcome to all our good things here at Chautauqua."

Fig. 10 **Lewis Miller** and **John Vincent** - sculptural images displayed before Rose Cottage, #2 Roberts, on Recognition Day.

Fig. 11 **The "Gingerbread Cottage"** (1891) - summer home of Pauline Fancher, author and former librarian at Smith Library.

The harmony of thought, as between the founders, is born out by the following quotation from John Heyl Vincent's Recognition Day address weeks later in that same year (1888):

"Now the doctrine which Chautauqua teaches is this, that every man has the right to be all that he can be, to know all that he can know, and to do all that he pleases to do—so long as being what he can be and knowing what he can know and doing what he pleases to do, does not keep another man from knowing all that he can know, being all that he can be and doing all that he pleases to do. And the Christian idea of the Chautauqua movement sees that the Christian elements enter into it as one of its essential features. It is the duty of every man to help every other man be all that he can be, know all that he can know and do all that he pleases to do under the aforesaid limitations. And position in life has nothing to do with it; a man is a man who has a man's motive, a man's purpose, a man's will and who bows reverently before God that he may worship Him and gain strength to help his neighbors."

Lewis Miller was President of the Chautauqua Assembly (not until re-chartered in 1902 did it become the Chautauqua Institution) until his death in New York City following surgery in 1899. His daughter, Mina, married Thomas Alva Edison, the great inventor. Since Edison was born in 1847, we might assume that the union took place at about the time Chautauqua was founded. Edison paid many summer visits to the Lewis Miller Cottage which overlooks what is now Miller Park where the original, open 'amphitheatre' was located. It is said that this cottage, constructed of lumber pre-cut in Akron, Ohio—hence one of the earliest pre-fabricated houses in America—was rushed to completion in time for President Ulysses S. Grant's visit to Chautauqua in the summer of 1875. The cottage was eventually inherited by Mina Edison who, in 1922, greatly modified and updated it without compromising, in the least, its original appearance (cf. photos p. 24-27).

In the very year of the Recognition Day address from which we have quoted (i.e. 1888) John Heyl Vincent was elected Bishop of the Methodist Episcopal Church - a post from which he retired in 1904. His Chautauqua summer residence, located on South Lake Drive at the corner of Peck Street, was lost in a fire in 1901. This site and his life are now commemorated by the quite lovely Bishop's Garden. Vincent passed away in his 88th year in 1920. Jacob Miller, brother of Lewis, built one of Chautauqua's most flambouyant victorian cottages on a site several lots north of Vincent's which was razed circa 1929 to make way for the Chautauqua Women's Club at 30 S. Lake Drive.

In the early years most of those attending the Chautauqua Assembly lived in tents. These were either brought along or, in some instances, fabricated on the premises. A number of the quaintest homes on the grounds today were built on tent platforms. Among these are most of the attractive, little cottages facing Miller Park on its north side (Fig. 12), also the so-called "Gingerbread" cottage (1891) at the corner of Wythe and James Avenues (Fig. 11) and the charming "Peony Cottage" (1895) located at 22 Center Avenue (Fig. 13). Originally, a striped tent was erected on the extended, righthand porch deck of the Lewis Miller cottage as a men's dormitory. Additionally, large tents, some acquired from the Philadelphia Centennial in 1876-77, were erected on the high ground, now Bestor Plaza, and used for various assemblies.

In 1878, four years after the founding of the Chautauqua Assembly, the CLSC or Chautauqua Learning and Science Circle was established. The CLSC program, for those who undertook it (the first class numbered eight thousand; by 1918 300,000 were enrolled), involved the reading of four prescribed books annually for a period of four years, discussing them within one's own, local reading circle and responding satisfactorily to questionnaires from Chautauqua. Those who satisfactorily completed this program, which continues to this day, received diplomas and were graduated ("recognized") on Recognition Day.

In **Chautauqua Publications** (1934) a concise history by Arthur E. Bestor Jr., son of Chautauqua's longest tenured and most influential President (1915 - 1944), it is written:

> "Of all the educational experiments launched by John Vincent, the CLSC has been called the most influential . . . As it came to fruition at Chautauqua, the CLSC embodied the principal educational beliefs and motives that Vincent cherished throughout his life. He insisted that education never ended 'til the grave . . . he was convinced that a program of guided reading could at least initiate them to the "college outlook," give them a base-line from which to advance, and give their children the stimulation of a home where knowledge and educational ambition were respected."

Fig. 13 **The "Peony Cottage"** (1879) 22 Center Street, also built on a tent platform. (cf. also Fig. 173)

Fig 12. (below) Cottages lining Miller Park's north boundary which face the site of the original amphitheatre.

The CLSC was, at one and the same time, the first book club in America and, in a sense, the first correspondence school. It provided a welcome alternative to a college education when most had neither the funds nor the time to attend a college. To this day it is part of the aggregate in the cement that holds Chautauqua together and keeps it going. As Arthur Bestor Jr. points out in the aforementioned historical statement, the work of the Institution today consists of three branches:

1. the public program of lectures, operas, concerts and plays offered during the summer season.
2. the summer schools (in music, the fine and performing arts).
3. the home reading program of CLSC.

Pres. Arthur Eugene Bestor defined the ideals of Chautauqua in these praiseworthy terms:

"The Institution has stood for a conception of religion which includes . . . intellectual integrity, moral earnestness, appreciation of beauty and, above all, a social solidarity and obligation of service. Chautauqua has played an important part in breaking down the barriers between churches . . . and in shifting the emphasis from a personal, individualistic salvation to the concept "The World the subject of Salvation," from the idea of the Kingdom of God in a remote society in another world to that of a social order to be realized in this."

Fig. 14 "**Bayberry House**" (c. 1881) #6 Simpson

Fig. 15 "**The Albion**" (1885) #5 South Terrace

Fig. 16 **Maple Inn** - 8 Bowman Avenue, Tom and Linda Krueger hosts.

Fig. 17 **French Quarter** (1892), left, #15 Ames, right. The former is painted aqua with brown trim, the latter yellow and brown.

Color Plate - overleaf
Top - **Bestor Plaza,** Colonnade Building, Fountain sculpture by Fred Torrey.
Bottom - **Miller Bell Tower** at Fair Point, College Club Building.

PORCHES, WICKER, ROUTINE

If, upon entering Chautauqua, one is fortunate to have a reserved parking space, he ascends a short dirt path to a paved street, Massey Ave., which runs roughly north and south between the centrally located Main Gate and Longfellow Avenue at the southern extremity of the Institution's grounds. He then has the choice of several avenues - Cookman, Peck, Foster or Janes which, via Warren, leads through delightful Lincoln Park and Palestine Ave. to the heart of Chautauqua - the Amphitheatre and Bestor Square.

One immediately senses that he is entering a somewhat different "world" than that left behind in Buffalo, Cleveland, or Pittsburgh. By-in-large the architecture is that of a bygone era. At once he becomes aware of the ubiquitous front-porch often stacked two, three and four high, one above the other (Figs. 14-17). Earlier in this century, in the 'teens and twenties, the front porch was a popular appendage to most middle-class homes in America's cities and towns: perhaps particularly so in the middle west. One after the other, in strict linear formation - like soldiers at parade-dress - they lined the streets of residential neighborhoods. The Great Depression of the 1930's, and World War II which followed, brought residential building to a stand-still. When building resumed in the post-war era, it became fashionable in suburban neighborhoods to position the porch at the rear of the house; its occupants were motivated more by a desire for privacy than neighborliness; but there was something sociable, something typically American about the old front porch. One could relax thereon of a summer afternoon or evening and watch the world go by, for Americas' love affair with the automobile had not yet become totally pervasive.

The front porch, as it still exists in older sections of our cities and towns, and so conspicuously at Chautauqua, was a distinctly American innovation in architecture. Homes in European cities hide behind head-high stuccoed walls butting the sidewalk. Their living space is oriented inward; the wall assures privacy and a measure of protection. The American home, by contrast, was outward-looking. To be sure, the gracious Georgian Colonial home sometimes had a grand portico, but this was more to impress visually than as an outdoor extension of the living space. The front porch, or veranda (a word borrowed from the Indian language) was not, actually, part of the Georgian or neo-classic tradition.

Any attempt to track down the origin of the front porch inevitably leads to Andrew Jackson Downing's **The Architecture of Country Houses** first published in 1850. Downing (1815 - 1852) was first and basically a landscape architect, however, he published several books on house design and building practices, of which the title cited was the last and most comprehensive, and which greatly influenced the course of American architecture for decades. Of his Design Number X, a bracketed cottage **with veranda**, Downing has this to say:

Fig. 18 **The Baird-Wineman Cottage** - Bishop's Garden in the foreground.

"The larger expression of domestic enjoyment is conveyed by the veranda or piazza. In a cool climate, like that of England, the veranda is a feature of little importance; and the same thing is true in a considerable degree to the northern part of New England. But over almost the whole extent of the United States a veranda is a positive luxury in all the warmer parts of the year, since in mid-summer it is a lounging spot, a resting place, a social resort for the whole family at certain hours of the day."

Another possible origin of the front porch, not mentioned in the literature, stems from the Greek Revival house as it evolved in this country. In rural situations as well as in the smaller towns of our country, the Greek Revival house was, at first, a small temple block with its gable end oriented to the highway. Ultimately, this simple temple block sprouted recessed, lateral wings as the family became more affluent and spacial needs increased. It then became popular to create a porch in the angle between the temple block and the lateral appendage. In northeastern Ohio this configuration is referred to as the "Western Reserve" style, but it is by no means limited to Ohio.

The visitor, as he strolls towards the Amphitheatre and Bestor Square, will observe that the Chautauqua porch is furnished with items popular in by-gone days—perhaps a slat-backed, oak swing suspended from the ceiling by a galvanized iron chain, more often wooden chairs and rockers "upholstered" with fiber rush, sometimes a white wicker flower-stand with ferns. From a somewhat later period he sees an occasional metal "glider," popular in the nineteen forties and fifties, but which now has all but vanished from the urban scene. Window-boxes planted with geranium, petunia and impatiens are suspended or otherwise affixed to the porch rail; hanging fuschias accent the air space between lathe-turned porch posts.

Sturdy, old-fashioned wicker, passed from one generation to the next, is employed profusely, inside and out, at Chautauqua. It is doubtful that a greater concentration of 'vintage' wicker furniture could be found anywhere in America. Observing a few wicker pieces in a local (Chagrin Falls, O.) antique shop, my wife commented on all the wicker seen at Chautauqua. "Oh yes," the proprietress said, "we just shipped half a dozen pieces to Chautauqua." Old wicker, it seems, finds its way to Chautauqua even as old elephants, when their time has come, are said to find their way to elephant grave-yards.

Before one has spent many hours in Chautauqua he becomes aware of the quiet orderliness of the place despite the fact that on any given day during the summer season there may be five thousand or more people on the tightly confined grounds. This is due, in part, to the limitation on auto traffic and parking within the Institution's confines, also to the fact that construction, with its attendent hammering, sawing and clatter is not permitted in season, and, finally, to the generally good manners and politeness of Chautauquans. Because of the preponderance of wooden structures, there is an extraordinary amount of painting in progress in the weeks preceding D-day (day season commences) which then continues, to a lesser degree, into the season. The place is a professional painter's delight!

One notices, too, that the American flag is widely displayed by home-owners throughout the season as if to underscore the fact that Chautauqua is indeed an "American Institution." Also, that the close-packed Village is set in a mature beech, maple and oak forest - the cover of which adds to the feeling of intimacy one experiences. Trees are an important, not-to-be-overlooked, element of Chautauqua's charm; visualize Chautauqua without them!

A typical Chautauqua day commences with a visit to the Book Store to secure a daily paper (**Plain Dealer, Post Gazette** etc.) and the **Chautauqua Daily.** The latter's "To-day" column and timely articles are indispensible in scheduling one's activities from the multiple daily offerings. Between nine and ten-thirty in the morning, the plaza before the post office with its picturesque kiosks becomes a lively place (Fig. 21, there is no mail delivery from the 14722 ZIP code). The ten forty-five AM lecture at the Amphitheatre is a highlight of every week-day; hundreds 'migrate', via the "Brick Walk", to this marvelous ninety-year-old facility about which we will have more to say later on. The subject of the day, as earlier noted, may deal with national affairs, with science and health, with literature, or with business and economic affairs - each addressed by speakers with differing viewpoints for a solid week.

Fig. 19 **Wilder Cottage** (c. 1887) #8 Miller Park - its typically Chautauquan porch furnished with old wicker.

Fig. 20 **String group performs**, impromptu, on Bestor Plaza of a summer evening.

At noon, if one is eager, he may elect to attend a brown-bag, art, lecture-demonstration at the Arts and Crafts Center or, at one o'clock, a docent tour of the Art Association Gallery. At two in the afternoon most will once again perambulate the Brick Walk (Fig. 54) to the Hall of Philosophy where, under the aegis of the Department of Religion, the subject will be concerned with some philosophical or moral issue. At three PM one may elect to attend an illustrated talk at Smith-Wilkes Hall sponsored by the Bird, Tree and Garden Club, or alternatively, an art lecture by Revington Arthur in the diminutive Octagon building. All may then be 'topped-off' at five with a travelogue by indefatiguable Kenneth Close. Time out for dinner!

There is never a dull evening at Chautauqua; they follow a pattern: Monday evenings at eight-thirty the Chautauqua Festival Orchestra composed of collegiate or garduate music students, holds forth; Tuesdays, Thursdays and Saturdays the professional Chautauqua Symphony performs - often with a featured soloist, Wednesday evening it might be Heloise, Geraldine Fitzgerald, Rod McKuen or other celebrity; Fridays are reserved for big-band and/or big-name entertainers - the likes of Harry Bellafonte, Ray Charles, Melissa Manchester - all performances are attended by thousands. Most, in residence, will attend as many concerts during a month at Chautauqua as in a year wherever home may be - so accessible is the Amphitheatre.

While the above has been transpiring, music students are daily practicing, rehearsing and perfecting their techniques; aspiring artists, sculptors, weavers, potters and metal-smiths, too, - many on scholarships - are 'doing-their-thing' at the Arts and Crafts Center. Chautauqua is a very creative place. It is, indeed, reassuring, to seniors such as this writer, to see so many young people seriously going about their business daily. Furthermore, it is not uncommon, and most pleasurable of an early summer evening, to encounter a youthful woodwind ensemble or string group informally performing on Bestor Plaza (Fig. 20). Music is in the air!

From many of the photographs contained herein one might erroneously conclude that Chautauqua is for elders. Seniors do predominate at the morning and afternoon lectures because at these hours music students are at practice sessions and the entire education program is in session. The fact is that Chautauqua attracts a great many families with young children; many have been coming for four, five and six generations. Their children, five years and upwards, attend summer camp programs mornings and afternoons. As Chautauqua offers something for every interest, so too it offers something for every age . . . a total family experience! Good people from the Julliard and Eastman Schools of Music, from Oberlin and elsewhere, are increasingly finding their way to Chautauqua for a summer music experience. Increasingly, retirees from Florida are partaking of the stimulation and pleasure of Chautauqua while escaping the torrid

Fig. 21 **Kiosks before the Post Office** - a lively place of rendevous, mornings.

summer heat prevailing at their winter condominiums. There is, in fact, such a demand for accommodations within the confines of the Institution today that the finite number of housing units is strained to accommodate all who wish to attend at reasonable rates. This is leading some to fear that Chautauqua may one day become exclusively a rich man's domain.

Fig. 22 **Docent tour** of the Art Association Gallery, a one o'clock election.

23

TENTING, LEWIS MILLER COTTAGE

Fig. 23 **Lewis Miller Cottage:** rear garden facade.

In considering the residential architecture, of which the largest part of the built community is comprised, one needs bear in mind that Chautauqua is, and has always been, a seasonal summer settlement. The vast majority of its dwellings are not winterized; its hotels and boarding houses are mostly closed for all but two or, at most, three months of the year. However, over the past decade there has been an increasing tendency among cottage owners to insulate and install heating systems. Chautauqua's cottages are, therefore, for the most part, second homes - less pretentious, less high-styled than one would expect to find in principal residences of their time in the city.

Chautauqua continues to evolve, to change and to grow. One hundred years ago, when in its infancy, it was, as has been noted, quite common to "tent" during the term of the 'assembly.' The **Chautauquan Daily** in a July, 1983 "100 Years Ago" column reminds us of those times:

"Tents can be rented by giving ten days notice, at a scale of prices given below. Parties bringing their own tents can rent ground for them at for one to five dollars, according to the size and style of tent and the expense of having it laid (which will be done by the Association if desired) will be about the same. Most of the necessary items of room furniture can be rented at the general office, at prices given below. Wood, ice and straw can be ordered at the same place. The bakery, dairy (with rich Chautauqua county milk and cream) the grocery and other supply stores, will fully meet all demand in their respective lines." Tent rates (including floor) -

Size	1 week	2 weeks	3 weeks	Add'l. weeks
9 x 12'	$ 6	$10	$13	$3
12 x 17'	$ 8	$14	$19	$4
16 x 24'	$12	$20	$26	$5

Rental price of furniture and bedding for Assembly season

Bedstead	$.90	Comforter	$.40
Single cot	.60	Bed tick	.50
Pillow	.15	Chair	.25 etc.

We quote further from the summer 1983 **Daily Chautauquan** "100 Years Ago" column for the light shed on early Chautauqua - housing:

"Many of the private cottages on the grounds are open for boarders and afford good and ample accommodations at reasonable rates, usually from five to ten dollars per week. Lodging can be obtained generally at 50¢/bed. CLSC, the great people's college, started but five years ago, has increased with such astonishing rapidity that now between thirty and forty thousand persons are connected with it and the new class (1886) numbers 12,000 . . ."

There is no tenting on the grounds today, but, as we have noted, a number of the more charming cottages are built on former tent-platforms.

The Lewis Miller Cottage (Fig. 24), completed in the summer of 1875, just in time to receive Pres. Ulysses S. Grant, is one of the very oldest and, at the same time, one of the most interesting cottages on the grounds. It is located at #28 Miller Park, near the Lake, facing the site occupied by the original Amphitheatre. It is known to have been constructed of timbers precut in Akron, Ohio - Miller's home town - then shipped to Chautauqua. Originally its ground floor contained a front parlor and at least one, perhaps two, smaller rooms; the second floor was used as a dormitory for ladies. Early photographs show a boldly striped tent installed on an extension of the front porch (at right) which was used as a men's dormitory. The walls of the Miller cottage are one board in thickness with the criss-cross members serving as structural supports. It was more usual at this time to build with the so-called "ballon-frame" introduced at mid-century (equi-distant studs of pre-cut, sized dimensions). The Miller cottage is therefore, of unique, and in some respects, advanced design; it is certainly one of the earliest and oldest pre-fabricated structures extant in the United States.

Stylistically, the cottage suggests a Swiss Chalet. Cottages in the Swiss mode were espoused by Andrew Jackson Downing in his **Architecture of Country Houses**. His cottage design #XI details the Swiss cottage which he says:

". . . may be considered the most picturesque of all dwellings built of wood. Bold and striking in outline, especially for its widely projecting roof which is perculiarly adopted to a snowy country . . . rustic and quaint in ornaments and details, it seems especially adapted to the wild and romantic scenery where it originated . . .

The true site for the Swiss cottage is in a bold and mountainous country, or at the bottom of a wooded hill, or in a wild and picturesque valley. In such positions the architecture will have a spirit and meaning which will inspire every beholder with interest . . ."

Fig. 24 **Lewis Miller Cottage** (1875) #28 Miller Park.

The considerably larger cottage pictured by Downing features the broad, bracketed eaves seen in the Miller cottage, also bracket-supported porches extending the width of the structure. A picturesque Swiss cottage is also featured in Fig. 63 of Downing's book. The Miller Cottage has stylistic elements which architectural historians today consider characteristic of the then emergent "stick style"* - most particularly its criss-cross members.

The Miller Cottage, designated a National Historic Landmark in 1966, has important historic associations. As we have seen Pres. Grant visited it upon completion in 1875. Thomas Alva Edison who married Lewis Miller's daughter, Mina, must have visited the cottage many times; he was a member of the 1930 CLSC class. Edison's friend, Henry Ford and his wife, were guests at the cottage and it is a certainty that Pres. James A. Garfield was received there in 1880 when, in an address at Palestine Park, he said, "It has been the struggle of the world to gain more liesure, but it was left to Chautauqua to show us how to use it.". Edison's son, Charles, governor of New Jersey and a former Navy Secretary under Franklin D. Roosevelt, was present when the cottage was designated a National Landmark in 1966.

In 1922 Mina Edison carried out extensive revisions and additions to the cottage including the installation of a kitchen wing and bedroom. She remodelled the ground-floor so that the parlor now occupies the entire floor area. The former second-floor ladies dormitory was partitioned into separate bedrooms. She laid out the rear garden and caused two adjoining cottages to be demolished. Miller Cottage is owned today by Mrs. Edward Arnn of Louisville, Kentucky, a great grand-daughter of Lewis Miller. She has maintained the ground-floor parlor and the garden exactly as it was furnished by Mina Miller Edison who passed on in 1947 (Figs. 23, 26)

The Lewis Miller cottage is painted a medium to light gray. It is of interest to note that throughout the Greek Revival period (1825 - 1850) white was the preferred color for house painting. Thereafter, in Victorian times, white was eschewed. Once again, the publication of **The Architecture of Country Houses**, establishing Andrew Jackson Downing as a foremost authority on taste in building, had much to do with this. We quote him in the matter of exterior house color:

"No person of taste, who gives the subject the least consideration is, however, guilty of the mistake of painting or coloring country houses white . . . Our first objection to white is that it is glaring and conspicuous . . . Our second objection is that it does not harmonize with the country and thereby mars the effect of the rural landscape . . . landscape painters always studiously avoid the introduction of white in their buildings and give them instead some neutral tint . . .

*This appellation, widely accepted, was made by Vincent J. Scully in his **The Stick Style and the Shingle Style** - Yale University Press

Fig. 25 **Marker**, below Amphitheatre, commemorating John Heyl Vincent.

"No one is successful in rural improvements who does not study nature and take her for the basis of his practice . . . The practical rule which should be deduced from this is to avoid all those colors which nature avoids . . . We think that, in the beginning, the color of all buildings in the country should be those of soft and quiet shades called neutral tints, such as fawn, drab, gray, brown, etc. and that all positive colors such as white, yellow, red, blue, black, etc. should be avoided; neutral tints being those drawn from nature . . . (pages 198 - 203)"

Fig. 26 **Lewis Miller Cottage:** parlor interior unchanged since redecorated by Mina Miller Edison in 1922.

Fig. 27

Fig. 28

INSTITUTIONAL ARCHITECTURE

It seems appropriate, before proceeding further with consideration of Chautauqua's domestic architecture, to consider her important Institutional buildings. The most important of these is the **Amphitheatre** - the focus of much that goes on at Chautauqua. The original amphitheatre, as we have earlier noted, was located in what is now Miller Park where the terrain slopes gently to Lake Chautauqua. Seating consisted of rows of backless benches (boards) which, by 1876, were protected from the elements by a pavilion-type tent—perhaps acquired from the Philadelphia Centennial of 1876. The first hard-roofed amphitheatre was located further up the hill in the ravine which, requiring a minimum of excavation and smoothing, was ideally suited to the purpose and so serves to this day. This first structure, dedicated on August 2, 1879, covered an area of 145' x 180'. Its overhead canopy was supported by 55 wooden pillars held in place by 330 braces. Thirty-six thousand board feet of lumber were required in its construction which, when completed, was covered with a white asbestos material. Mr. W. W. Calvin was the architect. There were difficulties with this structure; the roof leaked, the large number of supporting, wooden columns interferred with the view from many seats and rain falling on its roof made a disturbing, if not deafening, noise, also in the height of the season its capacity was over-taxed.

In the summer of 1892, little more than a dozen years later, the trustees approved an entirely new amphitheatre which seemed most practical when comparisons were made with the cost of rebuilding the existing structure. Pres. Lewis Miller, largely responsible for the plan and financing of the original amphitheatre, played a major role, once again, in the building of its successor. Plans envisioned the present amphitheatre, 180' long x 160' in width, having a pitched roof supported by bridge-type trusses bearing in turn on a minimum number of steel posts (only twenty of these are visible). The spacing of the posts is such that there is a central space 160' x 100' without columnar support. The lateral-extending, under-surface of the vast roof is supported at its eaves by bracketed, wooden posts (cf. Fig. 28). The structure was fitted-out with solid-backed wooden benches, providing excellent visibility as, in tiers, they descend towards the stage. The leak-free roof is said to be sheathed with iron shingles. Whatever the roofing may be, sound is deadened so that programs can be heard even in a moderately heavy rainstorm. Within, the tongue-and-grooved, wooden ceiling, arched over the great, unsupported central space, seals the sound-deadening air space occupied by the roof-bearing trusses. Accoustically, wood is among the best of all materials as born out by the Amphitheatre's excellent auditory characteristics. An interesting phenomena at Chautauqua's morning lectures and evening symphonies is the multitude of folks converging on the Amphitheatre carrying foam cushions. Considering the hard, wooden seats

Fig. 29 **Bowman Avenue vista** - the "Aldine" at left.

opposite page
Fig. 27 **Amphitheatre:** Audience assembles for a concert.

Fig. 28 **Amphitheatre:** Its vast roof is supported at the eaves by bracketed posts.

29

these almost become a necessity for favoring the derrière and have created a market for Chautauqua-inscribed, portable pillows.

The installation of the Massey organ, July 12, 1907, a memorial to Hart A. Massey by his family, necessitated the enlargement and rearrangement of the "working end" of the Amphitheatre (the son of the donor, Chester D. Massey, was a brother-in-law of Bishop Vincent and father of Raymond Massey, the noted actor). Modifications to the original choir-loft seating were made in 1921. In 1954 the platform (stage) was widened, new rooms were provided for visiting performers as well as storage of instruments and sanitary purposes, also a new roof covering was installed. The year 1964 saw a new cement floor cast in place; in 1967 bleachers seating 500 persons were added and in 1978 the roof trusses were reinforced.

The Amphitheatre is a truly remarkable structure. It serves as well today as when constructed over ninety years ago. Is there another such facility in America of which this could be said? It seats between six and seven thousand persons quite comfortably; occasionally, for certain big-name entertainment, as many as ten thousand persons may be packed into the Amphitheatre and standing-room in the enclosure which surrounds it. The latter, consisting of a well-designed contemporary metal rail supported at intervals by brick piers, is an environmentally enhancing improvement carried out with funds from the Second Century campaign (cf. Fig. 28). If one is equipped with his foam pillow, from all other aspects it is as pleasant to attend a symphony in Chautauqua's 90-year old Amphitheatre as in the contemporary Cleveland Orchestra's Blossom Music Center despite all that has been learned in the intervening years . . . and you can walk home! The Amphitheatre is almost continuously in use during daylight hours, if not for scheduled programs for rehearsals. The popular "Sunday at Chautauqua" religious services are held in the Amphitheatre weekly in season. Few podiums in the land have hosted as many noted performers and speakers.

Board Chairman Howard Gibbs made these remarks upon the repainting of the Amphitheatre in July of 1982:

"In essence the Amphitheatre is a place of repose, reflection and renewal - a place to learn, to question, to share; a place where history is made."

Art student sketching of a morning in Miller Park. Arcade Building in the background.

Fig. 30 **Amphitheatre:** Audience departs following
a morning lecture.

Fig. 31 **Amphitheatre:** Off-season aspect of one
quadrant.

Fig. 33 **Amphitheatre and Screen House** viewed from Smith Library.

Fig. 34 **Chautauqua Amphitheatre** (1893), one of two main, gate entrances.

The **Hall of Philosophy** has been called the second most important building on the grounds - second only to the Amphitheatre. It is, along with Norton Memorial Hall, one of the most aesthetically pleasing. President Robert Hesse has aptly referred to it as "a Chautauqua treasure." As a student and great appreciator of classical Greek architecture, I was awed by the beauty of this structure upon my first encounter with it; each revisitation evokes an aesthetic response. Occupying an entire, wooded block in which it rests like a jewel in a velvet lined box, the Hall of Philosophy takes the form of a quadrastyle, Doric temple which is to say that it is fronted with four columns on its smaller dimension - the lateral colonnades each having six columns for a total of sixteen. (We have counted each corner post twice).

Not hide-bound by tradition and the strict architectural conventions of the Doric temple, in which the columns are set on a platform or stylobate three steps above ground level, architect Albert Kelsey of Philadelphia actually depresses the Hall's floor a step or two with the very beneficial result that persons sitting on peripheral benches are able to view the podium without obstruction. The spacing of the columns, particularly at the ends, seems somewhat greater than that which the Greeks would have prescribed, but here again Kelsey's deviation provides adequate support for the trussed, wooden roof which, in the fully developed temple of the Classical period, would have been fabricated of much heavier stone. Happily, the additional space between columns frames dreamy vistas of the many great trees in the environs which one, more or less consciously, admires as he concentrates on the speaker's text. The columns have a pleasing taper, from top to bottom, but do not exhibit the entasis, or mid-section swelling, which appeared as one of the optical refinements of this ancient Greek temple style. Finally, it might be observed that the Greek Temple made provision for a walled cella within the peristyle which housed the cult statue to whom the Temple was dedicated and named. Such a room, of course, would have defeated the use which the Hall of Philosophy serves. An important and interesting distinction as between Chautauqua's Hall and the Athenian Temple is that the Greek Temple was intended to be viewed by the populace from the outside - only a few priests being admitted to its inner sanctum - while Chautauqua's "treasure" is designed to accommodate an audience of one thousand persons. Never-the-less, using the Greek, Doric temple as a model and an inspiration, architect Kelsey has given us an exceedingly useful, practical and beautiful, open-air auditorium.

Kelsey's structure, the cornerstone for which was placed in 1903 but which was not completed until 1906, (there was an interim during which the foundation was covered by a tent) replaced a quite similar earlier temple of 1879 known as "The Hall in the Grove." This, too, was supported by sixteen columns, but these were square, and fashioned of wood, without the architectural nicities which characterize

Fig. 35 **The "Golden Arch"** (Hall of Philosophy in background)

overleaf
Fig. 36 **Hall of Philosophy:** Elie Wiesel addresses a capacity audience, July, 1983.

Fig. 37 **The Hall of Philosophy** (1906) - an open-air lecture center in the Greek mode.

Fig. 36

Fig. 37

the reasonably authentic, fluted, cast-concrete columns and capitals of its successor. The classical sculptor J. Massey Rhind collaborated with architect Kelsey and may have played a major role in the realization of the aesthetic result achieved in the present Hall. Boston landscape architect, Warren H. Manning, was retained to oversee its landscaping. At the distance from which this is written, it is believed that both the present Hall and its predecessor measure approximately 100' in length by 60' in width (as paced-off by the author).

In retrospect, it is somewhat surprising that the Greek temple form was selected as a model, in the first instance, even for the 1879 "Hall in the Grove," for the nation's infatuation with "things Greek," particularly Greek architecture, had largely spent itself by the early 1850's in favor of Tuscan, Gothic and Romanesque revival styles. In the nation at large, not until the turn of the century was there another neoclassic revival sparked by the eastern establishment's influence upon the architecture of the 1893 Chicago World's Fair. What we have at Chautauqua, however, is so well-planned, so well situated, so appropriate to the forums held thereunder that to describe it as an anachronism seems inappropriate. It is rather a stroke of genius.

Fig. 38 **The Hall of Philosophy** - an oblique autumn aspect (cf. also Color Plate 2)

The roof timbers of the Hall of Philosophy are stained a dark brown which contrasts dramatically with its white, fluted, concrete columns. The roof slope adheres reasonably to Greek precedent, but the extending eaves are an understandable concession to its modern-day use. Four trusses of heavy timber, which in their construction suggest Japanese building methods, support the roof aided by the pediments at either end. The architraves, supported by the Doric column capitals, bear an incised, newly gilded Greek Key design on their exterior surfaces and a quadrifoil-design within. The customery metopes and tryglyphs are only suggested. Four-foot-high masonry pedestals opposite each corner of the Hall bear classical caldrons supported by tripods - gifts of one or more CLSC classes. These are lighted annually at the vesper, service preceding Recognition Day festivities. The whole ensemble is a fantastic concept which has, in capable hands, evolved over a century. In this day when most lectures and symposia are conducted indoors, this open-air pavilion at Chautauqua is novel, is indeed inspired.

The facility is shared mainly by the Department of Religion, which in season sponsors lectures each weekday afternoon at 2 p.m., and the Chautauqua Learning and Scientific Circle (CLSC) which schedules lectures by selected authors each Thursday afternoon at 3:15 P.M. - these presentations often being by writers whose books are required reading during the current year by CLSC participants. The CLSC Recognition Day (graduation) service takes place in the "Hall" each August. On this most august occasion of the Chautauqua calendar, the graduating class, accompanied by a colorful procession displaying the flags of all former classes, passes under the "Golden Arch," (Fig. 35) fronting on Fletcher Street, before solemnly ascending to the Hall and taking its preferred position before the podium. The concrete floor surrounding them bears the mosaic insignia of most, if not all, past classes (Fig. 40). Other Chautauqua organizations, including the Women's Club, make use of this extraordinary facility.

Fig. 40 **Hall of Philosophy:** detail of a CLSC mosaic.

Fig. 39 **Hall of Philosophy:** an overflow audience (the Hall seats 1,000)

37

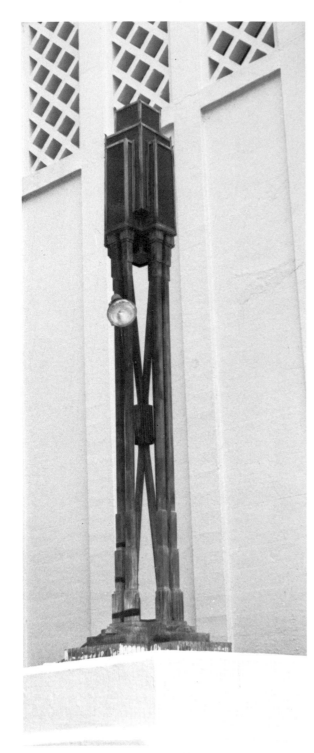

Fig. 41 **Lamp**, one of a pair flanking entrance to Norton Hall, is pure Art Deco

Norton Memorial Hall (Fig. 42) ranks very high among my favorite buildings at Chautauqua. I have the feeling, however, that this sentiment is not as enthusiastically shared by the majority of Chautauquans. Although built in 1929, almost two-thirds of a century ago, it is stylistically the most contemporary institutional building on the grounds - Bellinger Hall excluded (This relative modernity could explain what I perceive to be a general lack of enthusiasm for it in the prevailing traditional environment.) It is distinguished in that it incorporates more art in its design than any other Chautauqua building. This is due to the well-spring from which its design was derived . . . a sculptor's atelier. The building was the gift of Mrs. O. W. Norton of Chicago as a memorial to her husband and daughter. In seeking guidance for its design, it was quite natural that members of the family should have contacted Lorado Taft, a noted Chicago sculptor who had trained at the Ecole des Beaux Arts in Paris from 1880 to 1883, and had been a long-time instructor at the Art Institute of Chicago. In addition to the numerous, prestigious art societies to which Taft belonged, he was an honorary member of The American Institute of Architects. Taft referred the project of Otis F. Johnson, a young man who worked in his studio. It is said that Johnson's preliminary sketch is much the way the building looks today. Mr. Fred Torrey and his wife, Mabel, sculptors associated with Taft, designed the sculptural elements (Fig. 45) atop the piers flanking the structure's central facade; also the fountain sculpture now before the Post Office but which was originally designed for, and placed before, Norton Hall. Lorado Taft was aesthetic advisor throughout.

The modernistic style, so well represented by Norton Memorial Hall, received its impetus from the important Exposition des Arts Decoratifs held in Paris in 1925. This Exposition sparked modernistic designs in furniture, jewelry, art and architecture which, taking their cue from the Exposition's title, became known as Art Deco. In architecture, ornament in low relief in combination with flat, planal surfaces, is an important distinguishing feature of the style. This is exactly what we see in Norton Hall. I would suggest that Norton Hall, tucked away in relatively remote Chautauqua, is one of the unrecognized jewels of its period and design in America. The large, rectangular relief (sculpture) at the upper left hand corner of the facade, with a nude at its center, depicts "The Birth of Beauty"; that in the upper right hand corner is entitled "Moods of Music." The squarish relief panels of Pan, god of forests, pastures, flocks, and shepherds, forming an integral part of the proscenium within, were executed by Elizabeth Hazeltine, at the time a faculty member at The Art Institute of Chicago. Between these elements, in a most artistic, sculptural script, is the axiom "All Passes-Art Alone Endures" - attributed to Theophile Gautier. Norton Hall is a statement by a later day "Chicago School" (the Lorado Taft atelier) in a more modern style. Consider the tall, artistic, bronze, lamp stanchions

(Fig. 41) flanking the broad entrance stair—thoughtfully conceived, pure Art Deco.

Norton Memorial Hall was built at a cost of $140,000; it seats 1,367 persons (two-thirds in the orchestra, one-third in the balcony). It measures 83' x 143' with a height (at the front) of 40'. The proscenium is 38' x 20' in height - the stage 28' in depth. There is a basement only under the stage. Cast against wooden forms, (the timber lines of which can be faintly seen at close range) the Hall is considered to be one of the first, poured in situ, monolithic buidings in the Eastern United States. Thus, it is a significant building from a technical standpoint as well as aesthetically. The relief sculptures, too, were integrally cast against an appropriate mould. Virtually untouched since its construction sixty-four years ago, there are extensive plans afoot to restore and modernize the building. As it appears today Norton Hall is a very pale pink in color while its entrance loggia is painted a delicious lavender. At the first performance to be held in the Hall Taft said:

"I am reminded of the statement that art is the ark of the covenant in which all the ideals and revelations of beauty came before the people, and as I stand here I have a realization of what this is to mean to Chautauqua . . . The fundamental in art is that there is a hint of eternity."

Lorado Taft passed away on October 30, 1931.

Fig. 42 **Norton Memorial Hall** (1929) - an Art Deco "treasure" for the performing arts at Chautauqua.

Fig. 43

Fig. 44

Fig. 45

Fig. 46 **Smith-Wilkes Hall** (1924) - versatile, open air lecture hall and performing facility.

Summer at Chautauqua is largely an outdoor experience. The morning lectures at the Amphitheatre are, as we have earlier noted, a highlight of each day. One enjoys these essentially in the open with only a roof to shade and protect oneself from the occasional rainy day. When not focusing on the speaker, one's eyes are free to wander beyond the Amphitheatre's peripheral, bracketed posts to the United Presbyterian House on the one hand, or the Church of Christ headquarters on the other and all the foliage in between. The place is open to sunlight and to fresh air.

The same is true of The Hall of Philosophy, the center of activity each afternoon. Here one's eyes can roam in all directions; there are no walls to fix the limits of one's vision. The aesthetics of the environment - the architecture of the Hall itself, surrounded by the shaded, woodland grove in which it is situated - work to open one's heart and mind to whatever the speaker has to say before he has uttered a word. This place, too, is open to the sunlight and to fresh air.

There is still another open meeting-place at Chautauqua - namely **Smith-Wilkes Hall** (Fig. 46). Situated slightly south of the Amphitheatre, it may be approached by means of an intimate walk which skirts the United Presbyterian House and the Carnahan-Jackson Memorial Garden. Smith-Wilkes, the gift of Mrs. C.M. Wilkes as headquarters for the Chautauqua Bird, Tree and Garden Club, was built in 1924 - sixty years ago as this is written! It comes alive at 3:15 most weekday afternoons with presentations, often augmented by slides, mostly dealing with the natural environment. During the summer of 1983 Chautauquans were enlightened on bats which, it seems, control the mosquito population on Chautauqua's shores; on owls, on certain animal's ability to perceive color. They were inspired by a synchronized, poetic dialogue of word and picture descriptive of Thoreau's Walden (produced by two Chautauquans), and if they tarried long enough - might yet have enjoyed a travelog by the irrepressible Kenneth Close.

opposite page
Fig. 43 **Norton Memorial Hall** - a complementary, vertical oblique aspect.

Fig. 44 **Norton Memorial Hall** - the proscenium. "All Passes-Art Alone Endures" - attributed to Theophile Gautier.

Fig. 45 **Norton Memorial Hall** relief sculptures: that at left entitled "The Birth of Beauty", at right "Moods of Music"

Fig. 47 **CLSC Alumni Hall** - late Victorian fireplace ensemble in trustees room. Tall desk was the gift of Julius King.

opposite page
Fig. 48 **CLSC Alumni Hall** (1892) - the special province of CLSC graduates.

Smith-Wilkes, octagonal in form, is constructed of buff, tapestry brick with brick pillars supporting the roof structure. These brick columns alternate with open spaces, approximately 7' x 10', around two thirds or more of the structure - there being a solid wall behind the stage. Here, again, the person in attendance enjoys the same openness, the same sunlight and fresh air as at the Amphitheatre or the Hall of Philosophy. Exceptionally well-fitting shades may be dropped in place to cover the openings when slides or movies are to be shown. Smith-Wilkes, on a split-level, is constructed like a small amphitheatre with five rows of permanent seating forming a "theatre-in-the-round." Built at a cost of $27,705 (1929 dollars), it seats almost 500 persons. It is an extremely versatile facility with an elevated stage preceded by a mini-arena (encircled by the seating) which can be used by musical groups, dancers etc.;—while the aforementioned provision for darkening makes a theatre of it. It is typically 'Chautauqua' for its openness to the out-of-doors.

Let us now amble back, my means of the Brick Walk, to the level, open space before the Hall of Philosophy. This might be called "CLSC Country" for, with the exception of the Hall of Christ, it is surrounded by buildings having to do with The Chautauqua Learning and Scientific Circle. The largest of these, directly opposite the Hall of Philosophy, is the **CLSC Alumni Hall** (Fig. 48) - the special province of those who have graduated from, or are participating in, one of its four-year reading programs. With its large, roofed veranda, extending the width of the building, one might mistake it for a country Inn. Alumni Hall was built in 1892 from designs by architect E. G. Hall of Jamestown, New York. (He was also architect for the Arcade - 1891). Within, an octagonal vestibule gives access to a spacious central hall. This is flanked by a dining room to the left and a trustees room to the right. All rooms are panelled with narrow, tongue and groove, pine boards which have darkened handsomely with age. The far left corner of the latter (i.e. the trustee's room) contains a fireplace (Fig. 47) quite typical of the period for its built-in, over-mantle mirror of bevelled glass, its attenuated, flanking, wooden columns and the Victorian character of the tesserae surrounding its fire-bed. The portrait above is that of Kate Kimball, CLSC Secretary from 1878, when she was 18, to her death in 1917. She must receive much credit for the success of the organization. In the opposite corner, a secretary (Fig. 49) given by Julius King is one of the more important furnishings. The hall and dining room are festooned with over 90 colorful banners representing CLSC classes from 1882 onward. These are removed once a year for the Recognition Day parade and graduation exercises (Fig. 190).

There are two buildings of interest on Cookman to the right of Alumni Hall as one faces the latter. These are **Oc-**

tagon House (Fig. 51) and **Pioneer Hall** (Fig. 50). The former was built by a group of Pittsburgh men in the early 1880's as their private clubhouse a decade before the idea for an Alumni Hall came to fruition. Now, equipped more or less like a one-room schoolhouse, its major use is for weekly Art Appreciation classes conducted by the perennial Revington Arthur and other occasional instructional purposes. The Octagon "fad" gained impetus through a book entitled **A Home for All or The Gravel and Octagon Mode of Building** published in the late 1840's by Orson Fowler. Fowler claimed that an octagon configuration enclosed more space with less wall-surface than the usual rectangle; also, in a home, one could follow the sun around its roughly circular porch. By 1880 the octagon mode had run its course. Chautauqua's singular specimen is roughly 8' to the side.

Pioneer Hall (Fig. 50) was built in 1885 at a cost of $1,200 by the first CLSC graduating class. It consists of one large room, approximately 30' x 30', the walls and ceiling of which are totally lined with the narrow, tongue-and-groove pine boards favored at the time; these have acquired an antique patina. The room has a fireplace at the left rear corner; there is no electricity. Maintained by the Class of 1963, it serves today as a museum of early Chautauqua artifacts. It is actually an attractive little building. Take note of the unusual dual pediments infilled with fish-scale, shingled sur-

Fig. 49 **Julius King Secretary**

Fig. 50 **Pioneer Hall** (1885) - recycled, it is now a museum of Chautauqua historic artifacts maintained by CLSC Class of 1963.

Fig. 51 **Octagon Building** (c. 1880) - originally a clubhouse, now a classroom.

44

faces, also the attractive open spindle course across the porch supported by posts with delicate, scroll-saw brackets. Pioneer Hall is open to visitation each Thursday afternoon, in season, following the CLSC sponsored program at the nearby Hall of Philosophy.

Let us now turn our attention to the **Hall of Christ** (Fig. 53), the off-white, brick, terra cotta and stone building with a grand classical portico in the Ionic order, which commands our attention upon entering this CLSC dominated open space beyond the Brick Walk. The Hall of Christ was envisaged as one of the most cherished building projects at Chautauqua. Founder John Vincent, according to Pres. Arthur Bestor (**Country History** - American Historical Society) conceived of it in these terms:

"A building of appropriate architecture devoted exclusively to the study of the man of Nazareth in which every day, at all hours, there shall be courses of study in the life, work, deeds and spirit and results of his life who 'spake as never man spake.' In this hall it is proposed to collect all engravings of Christ which the art of the ages puts within our reach, and a library of all the lives of Christ which have ever been written. It shall be a memorial hall with historic windows . . . Thus shall the central building of Chautauqua symbolize to the world the controlling aim and force of all her diverse ministeries."

Paul J. Pelz, who collaborated with J.L. Smithmeyer in designing The Library of Congress in Washington, was selected as architect for the Hall of Christ. He came fresh from involvement with the Congressional Library project which was consumated between 1889 and 1897. Two cornerstones, each weighing 1,000 pounds, which had been shipped from Jerusalem, were laid at Chautauqua on August 7th, 1900 . . . an auspicious year. A bible, photos of the founders - Lewis Miller and John Heyl Vincent - a Lafayette dollar and a daily newspaper were buried with these stones.

Its imposing portico is approached by a series of broad steps. The pediment, supported by four correct Ionic columns, depicts a book, the bible, with "arms" disseminating its message in all directions. The classical, trabeated entrance, suggesting a great mantel-piece in form, is flanked by niches intended to bear sculptured figures. Upon entering one is confronted by a rather stark nave terminating in an elevated alter and choir. Lateral appendages devoted to sacred art and the life of Christ suggest a transept but there is no crossing. The interior, quite void of decoration, is perhaps too well lighted by rows of clear glass windows.

To this point I have been lavish in my praise of Chautauqua buildings, but of this I feel that seldom have such high hopes missed the mark so sadly. Its design is quite in keeping with the Classical Revival very much "in" at the time. Furthermore, it is quite understandable that the leaders of Chautauqua, and those charged with its design, wished to build an imposing edifice appropriate for the greatest figure

Fig. 52 **Episcopal Chapel of the Good Shepherd** (c. 1898) - a little jewel tucked in the woods at the corner of Clark and Park.

in Christianity. My misgivings, I think - following a good deal of self-questioning - relate to the stark, cold, uninviting character of its interior. The problem is, I believe, that its possibilities are un-realized. It needs appropriate interior decoration - some sculpture, some art (murals), subdued lighting brought about, hopefully, by means of contemporary, stain-glass windows. These refinements were envisaged by Dr. Vincent. The facade niches cry for fulfillment. It is surprising, particularly at Chautauqua, that more in this direction has not been accomplished over three-quarters of a century.

There is, however, a little jewel tucked in the woods at the corner of Clark and Park streets - **The Episcopal Chapel of the Good Shepherd** (Fig. 52). The Chapel is actually quite close to the Hall of Christ, but can easily be overlooked if one is not alert. Simple and unsophisticated, it could eaisly 'wear' a thatched roof in good taste. Stylistically, we would call it "country Gothic." Its wall surfaces are sheathed with clapboard to the eaves - the gable itself being covered with shingle in a fish-scale pattern. The half-conical hood extending forward from the roof peak is a quaint and highly attractive feature of its facade. Take note of the hand-forged, strap hinges as you enter. Within, the wall surface is, once again, lined with the narrow, tongue-and-grooved pine boards so popular when it was constructed in the time frame 1895 - 1900. The wooden cathedral ceiling is sectioned between the rafters in an attractive manner. All windows are glazed with stained-glass which filters the light thereby creating a mood of religiosity. The large semi-circular window at the rear of the sanctuary (above the vestibule as seen in the photo), depicting a young woman stooping to admire a field of lilies, is particularly lovely; its caption reads "Consider the Lily." As so often happens, the architect of this lovely chapel is unknown. Though simple, unpretentious and recessive - not seeking our attention - this chapel is beautiful in the fullest sense of the word. It is very much in the restrained, down-to-earth spirit of Chautauqua; no wonder that it is a favorite subject for artists.

Fig. 53 **The Hall of Christ** (1900-09) - the fulfillment of a dream of founder John Heyl Vincent.

opposite page - above and below
Fig. 55 **The United Methodist House** (1888) 14 Pratt Ave. - Its broad veranda overlooks the re-developed plaza before the Amphitheatre.

Fig. 56 **Disciples of Christ House** (1904) - curious combination of a Classical portico fronting a Mansard-roofed, Second Empire block.

Fig. 54 **The Brick Walk** (also Clark Ave.) - well traversed passage-way from the Hall of Philosophy to Bestor Square and beyond.

While still under the spell of this delightful little church, let us retrace our steps, once again, past the equally inspiring Hall of Philosophy, and via the Brick Walk (Clark Avenue) amble back to Bestor Plaza. On our right, at the corner of Peck Street, we pass **Lutheran House** (1925) identified by its three great arches of earth-toned brick. It is difficult to assign any particular architectural style to it beyond faintly recalling the innovative colonnade of Brunelleschi's Foundling Hospital of 1419 AD in Florence, Italy. Further along, at the corner of James, we observe **The Disciples of Christ House** (Fig. 56), a curious combination of a neo-classical porch affixed to a Second Empire block. One wonders if they (porch and building) were conceived as a unit. As surmised they were not; the rear block was undoubtedly built in the 1880's. The portico was added at the turn of the century with wood donated by Cleveland's Teachout Lumber Co. transported largely by water to Chautauqua. Notwithstanding, the edifice adds to the general scene; architectural incongruities such as this, actually add to the quaintness of Chautauqua. Further on, in the recently re-designed open space before the Amphitheatre we notice **The United Methodist House** (1888; Fig. 55) fronted by a broad porch which affords a marvelous prospect of the passing parade. This building, too, is curious, the right and left-hand components, if carefully observed, give evidence, architecturally, of having been built at different times, which appears not to have been the case. (Note that the southern-most portion displays a classical vocabulary of forms - dentils, pilasters, mandorlas, etc. - not echoed in the other half.) No matter, it too, is part of the charm of Chautauqua.

Fig. 57 **Bestor Plaza** - Chautauqua's "Village Green" named to honor its longtime President, Arthur Eugene Bestor (1915-1944).

A few steps further on **Bestor Plaza** (Fig. 57) opens to us, named after Arthur E. Bestor whose presidency of Chautauqua Institution extended from 1915, - before our involvement in World War I, through the Great Depression of the 1930's, - virtually to the conclusion of World War II. A statement made by him, brought to my attention by Theodore Morrison's book **Chautauqua, A Center for Education, Religion and Arts in America** (page 237) greatly impresses me; it follows:

"This institution has stood for a conception of religion which includes intellectual integrity, moral earnestness, appreciation of beauty and, above all, social solidarity and obligation of service. Chautauqua has played an important role in breaking down the barriers between churches . . . and in shifting the emphasis from a personal, individualistic salvation to the concept - "the world the subject of salvation," from the idea of the Kingdom of God as a remote society in another world to that of a social order to be realized in this."

Oscar Remick, President from 1971 to 1977 seemed quite in tune with Bestor as judged by this statement quoted in the Epilogue of Morrison's book:

"Chautauqua, once characterized as typically American, will find its future by representing what is really human. This means that the narrowed indentification of Chautauqua with a certain segment of society, must give way to an openness, a universality, expressed in practice as well as in principal."

50

Bestor Plaza (Fig. 121) is, of course, the very heart of Chautauqua. At its center there is a fountain (Fig. 193) designed by Chicagoan Fred Torry who, as we have seen, executed the relief sculpture on the facade of Norton Hall; also the fount before the Post Office Building on the plaza's east side. The Bestor central fountain project was completed by him in 1946. **The Colonnade Building** (Fig. 57) which houses the Institution's offices on the second floor, was originally built at a cost of $35,000 in 1905, the then rebuilt following a fire in 1907 and restored after a second fire in 1961. Unfortunately, in its reconstruction the original attic was not duplicated, also the dual, curvilinear stairways within the recess of the colonnade leading to a balcony were omitted. The building, 90' x 173', suffers as a result of these deletions. To build the Colonnade, it was necessary to move the **Anne M. Kellogg Memorial Hall** (1889, Fig. 59) from the northwest corner of the Square to its present site on Pratt at Ramble. At that time Kellogg Hall housed a kindergarten and WCTU office on the first floor while handcraft courses for women were held on the second. It originally contained a lovely stained-glass window which was moved to #32 S. Lake Drive in August, 1924 on the fiftieth anniversary of the WCTU's founding at Chautauqua, when this lakefront location became the Union's headquarters. (In 1946, when the Haller family acquired #32 S. Lake the window was moved to WCTU National Headquarters in Chicago.) The ground-floor interior woodwork is quite interesting—particularly the tall, turned, mahogany, monolithic columns which support its ceiling. Kellogg Hall is ecclectic-defying specific stylistic designation.

Fig. 59 **Anne M. Kellogg Hall** (1889), Ramble at Pratt - summer school headquarters. Its ground-floor woodwork is of interest. (cf. also page 126)

Fig. 58 **Bestor Plaza** - guitar player entertains informally on a summer evening.

51

Fig. 60 **Pam Hallberg** of Miami University (Ohio) relaxes at Bestor Plaza fountain.

Fig. 61 **Florida Fountain** (frgrnd.), **Oriental Bazaar** (bkgrnd, 1889) at the SE corner of Bestor Square. The latter formerly housed the Institution's Administrative offices.

Fig. 62

Fig. 63

Smith Library (Fig. 63, 64), so important to this community of readers, occupies the entire south side of Bestor Plaza opposite the Colonnade Building. In the Georgian Revival style, it was built in 1931 with funds supplied by Mrs. A.M. Smith Wilkes. The Flemish bond of its brick and fine trabeated entrance are detailed in Fig. 64. The ground floor consists of one room beautifully illuminated by great windows on all sides (Fig. 63). It is a most pleasant space in which to browse or to engage in serious research. A dual stair on its central axis leads first to a landing with a Palladian window, then to the second floor where the Miller, Bestor and Edison collections are stored - also numerous historic and artistic artifacts owned by the Instition are on view.

Prior to 1931 there was a museum on the site of Smith Library. Through the good offices of Mr. J.E. Kittredge, Secretary of the Chautauqua Archeological Society, this museum acquired **Merneptah**, a 12th century BC royal charioteer and scribe to Ramses the Great (1290 - 1224 B.C.). The latter was discovered by Sir William Mathew Flinders Petrie (1853 - 1942), renouned British archeologist, who had lead an expedition to Defenneh and the Temple of the goddess Wadjet in the Nile Delta. Kittredge who was also an American representative of the Exploration Fund, sponsors of Petrie's expedition, was able to obtain the massive, black granite block (Merneptah) which for a time had been exhibited on the portico of the British Museum in London. The Chautauqua collection containing this invaluable bit of antiquity was dispersed in 1930 in preparation for the building of Smith Library. Merneptah's stony likeness was forgotten until, mirable dictu, in 1982 a crate was discovered in the former railroad station which now serves as the Chautauqua Gate (Fig. 84). Inside, the 3,000-year-old statue of Merneptah was found in the typical position of the Egyptian scribe—knees pulled up and held in position by his arms. The sculpture brought circa $300,000 in a Sotheby auction which certainly has not hurt the Institution's cash position. What a find!

The Chautauqua Book Store (Fig. 62) has had a migratory career. It appears, first, to have been located in the Arcade Building, then in what is now The Oriental Bazaar and also, at one time, in the Colonnade Building. For the past fifty years or more, however, it has occupied the English basement under the Post Office. In addition to its excellent collection of books, it also offers gift items and Chautauqua souvenirs. Vendor, also, of the **Daily Chautauquan** and Buffalo, Cleveland, New York and Pittsburgh dailies, it is one of the most important daily 'ports-of-call' for visitors and Chautauquans alike.

The **St. Elmo Hotel** (Fig. 67), an amalgam of buildings dating to 1890, occupies the northwest corner of Bestor Plaza between Ames and Vincent streets. Until recently it was a center of winter activities at Chautauqua, but is now no longer open in the winter. Its spacious lobby is a pleasant place and its dining-room a popular choice in season.

Fig. 64 **Smith Library** (1929) - its trabeated neoclassical entrance.

opposite page - top to bottom
Fig. 62 **The Chautauqua Book Store** - below the Post Office on Bestor Plaza. - A Chautauqua institution in itself!

Fig. 63 **Smith Library** - the inviting, main-floor reading-room is illuminated by no fewer than eighteen great windows.

55

Fig. 65 **Logan Dormitory** (c. 1890) fronting Bestor Square at Vincent - first a private cottage, then YWCA Hospitality House, now a student dormitory.

opposite page - top to bottom
Fig. 67 **St. Elmo Hotel** (1890 et sequitor) on Bestor Plaza. Vincent Street entrance to the venerable establishment.

Fig. 68 **Jewett House** (1880), Pratt at McClintock - another formerly private cottage in the Queen Anne style of its day, recycled to student dormitory use.

Logan Dormitory (Fig. 65, c. 1890), located opposite the St. Elmo at Pratt and Vincent, has served numerous purposes. Originally, it was the private home of the Martin family of Pittsburgh. Mrs. Lewis Lapham of New York City provided funds for the YWCA to acquire it in 1918-19 so that from 1922 it was operated as a YWCA Hospitality House. However, Mrs. Harry A. Logan of Warren, Pa. came forward with funds in 1965 which enabled the Institution to acquire it as a dormitory for summer school students. Its distinguishing features are the Palladian window in its gable and the articulated round tower with conical cap to its side. It might be described as mildly, aclectic Queen Anne style.
A **Christian Science House and Chapel** (Fig. 66) occupy the corner of Pratt and Center streets on Bestor Plaza.

The so-called Queen Anne style came into favor in England about 1870 and was introduced to America by two English buildings at the Philadelphia 1876 Centennial, which had a medieval quality about them. As the style was practiced in America to the end of the century, it was characterized by an irregularity of plan and massing, by multi-gabled roofs, overhangs, bay windows and round or polygonal turrets. Wall surfaces usually combined brick, on the ground floor, with shingle or clapboard above. There are a few houses at Chautauqua which truly can be said to be of the style. Perhaps the closest approach is that at #26 Cookman (Fig. 174) facing the Hall of Philosophy at the corner of Clark. **Jewett House**, too, (Fig. 68) at the Northeast corner of Pratt and McClintock exhibits Queen Anne forms in its multi-gabled, intersecting roof elements, and in the touch of what appears as half-timbering in its topmost gable. The combination of clapboard and shingle affords variety in its wall surfaces. It was built in 1880 as a girls' dormitory.

Fig. 66 **Christian Science House and Chapel** - corner of Pratt and Center.

opposite page - top right
Fig. 70 **Normal Hall** (1885) Pratt Ave. - Its facade gives little suggestion of the great space within supported by four massive wooden arches. An experimental theatre in 1983.

Let us now stroll northward on Pratt Ave. past Anne M. Kellogg Hall which we have noted and past the gothic **Hurlbut Memorial Church** (1931, Fig. 69), the interior of which is enhanced by Maritza Morgan's colorful painted panels, to **Normal Hall** (1885, Fig. 70) one of the oldest institutional buildings at Chautauqua and a very interesting one from an architectural standpoint. Are you old enough to remember that early in this century teachers were trained at a "normal school?" Well, this was a normal school for Sunday school teachers which was, of course, Chautauqua's reason-for-being at the time it was built. Today the wooden structure encloses one great space, or hall, fully sixty feet in length, and fifty feet in depth, the high, cathedral ceiling of which is supported by four, massive, laminated, wooden arches which spring from the ground and carry through to the roof peak (a second floor was torn out c. 1950). The walls are lined with the narrow, tongue-and-grooved pine boards which, as we have observed at Alumni Hall and Pioneer Hall, darken attractively with the passing years. These, of course, were never painted. High up in the north gable daylight is admitted through a large circular window divided by 'mullions' into pie-shaped segments. By 1930, no longer used for its original purpose, (it was a center for religious

Fig. 69 **Hurlbut Memorial Church** (1931) - essentially Gothic in style with art deco stained glass windows.

studies until the Hall of Christ was erected) Normal Hall became an adjunct to Norton Memorial Hall, its bright, new, and, in some respects overbearing neighbor to the north, which it served as a set-design studio and for rehearsals until, in the summer of 1983, it found use as an experimental theatre. As may be seen in the accompanying photograph, the porch appended to the great hall bears an interesting, sawn-art, geometric design in its gable.

When, or if, you attend a movie at Chautauqua take note of the beautiful hammer-beam truss ceiling of **Higgins Hall** erected in 1895 as a church to serve the needs of both Catholics and Protestants. Adapted for use as a cinema, it may well be the only artificially air-conditioned building on the grounds. Higgins Hall is located on Wythe Avenue near Hurst. To reach it we will have passed the **Ida A. Vanderbeck Chapel** (Fig. 71) built in 1963 by the International Order of the King's Sons and Daughters as a center for the spiritual activities of young people. This organization annually sponsors Chautauqua scholarships for one or more talented, English students in the arts. The Chapel, an attractive accent to the Chautauqua scene - identified by its small white spire - is in the Georgian Colonial style.

Fig. 71 **Ida A. Vanderbeck Chapel** (1963) Pratt Ave. - a spiritual center for young people.

opposite page - top
Fig. 73 **Arts and Crafts Quadrangle** - Revington Arthur, longtime painting instructor, gives a lecture-demonstration.

We now find ourselves within a short walk of the **Arts and Crafts Quadrangle** (Fig. 74). To reach it we pass by the Children's School (ages 2½ to 6 years), one Greek derived element of which, pictured in Fig. 78, reminds us of The Hall of Philosophy. Diagonally opposite we observe the multi-gabled **Hall of Education,** (Fig. 72) originally built on Pratt Street in 1898 and moved to its present location in 1911. Sheathed in brown shingles with contrasting white trim, it blends well with its neighbors but is rather odd stylistically. The Hall of Education was formed in 1911 from the union of two formerly separate structures. As noted elsewhere herein, considering the pent roofs, etc., it is a fair assumption that architect E.G. Hall, designer of CLSC Alumni Hall and the Arcade, did this as well. In season, illustrated art presentations are held in an upstairs classroom. The Hall, as it existed in 1983, is a likely (and worthy) candidate for some Second Century restoration funds.

The **Arts and Crafts Quadrangle** (Fig. 74-77), also known as The Art Center, enjoys a beautiful vista of Lake Chautauqua from its perch on "College Hill" - the highest point on the grounds. It was designed in 1909 by Henry Turner Bailey, while he was director of Chautauqua's summer art program. A native of North Scituate, Mass., Mr. Bailey came to Cleveland in the early 1920's to become head of The Cleveland School of Art. The Bailey family has figured pro-

Fig. 72 **Hall of Education** (1898) - located on the slope of College Hill, contains classrooms for summer-school courses and art lectures.

minently in Chautauqua affairs: daughter-in-law Helen M. Bailey, as a young woman, c. 1920, operated the original art and craft shop in the Colonnade Building; son Jack Bailey is a current trustee of the Institution. The Quadrangle is a complex of studios, in linear arrangement, each given to a separate discipline including painting, sculpture, ceramics, jewelry design, weaving, etc. Long and low, its lateral wings forming an open-ended courtyard, the brown shingle-sheathed structure is fronted by a covered gallery or colonnade, supported by white, cast concrete columns; this unifies the complex while enhancing its aesthetics. The many windows which open to this sheltered colonnade, together with those at the rear, give the studios something of the quality of open air workshops. The Quadrangle is a particularly lively place during classes on summer mornings - attended by persons whose age ranges from collegians to retirees (Fig. 183). Here one commences to sense the creativity which is part of the Chautauqua summer experience. Through a grant from the Helen Temple Logan trust, the Arts and Crafts Center has recently (1982 - 83) been restored (new roof, new paint, relaid brick walls, new drainage system) and may be expected to serve well into the 21st century.

Fig. 74 **Arts and Crafts Quadrangle** (1909) on "College Hill" houses studios in painting, ceramics, sculpture, weaving and jewelry making - all opening on the gallery.

Fig. 75 **Arts and Crafts Quadrangle** - a potter at the wheel. From window before him, he overlooks Lake Chautauqua.

Fig. 76 **Arts and Crafts Quadrangle** - Christine Yocca plans project in the weaving studio.

The Sherwood Piano Studio (Fig. 79), located across Hedding Ave. from The Art Center, fronts on Palestine Ave.; it closely resembles the latter in its general appearance. The colonnade which partially surrounds it would certainly seem to have been fashioned by the same hand. Sherwood Studio was built in 1912 as a memorial to William H. Sherwood, first head of the piano department at the Music School. It is used for piano instruction, master classes and recitals. It was reconditioned in 1966 through the generosity of Rena Munger Aldredge. (Earlier, during his lifetime, the Sherwood Studio occupied the top floor of the Arcade Building). This typically Chautauquan, vernacular style with brown-stained, shingle wall-covering and white or cream trim is echoed in The Lodge (Fig. 80), and the Lincoln Dormitory, both located nearby. Belinger Hall (1973 - 74), a combination dormitory, refectory and lounge for summer students, located at the northern extremity of Hedding Ave., is one of the newer additions to the grounds.

Fig. 77 **Arts and Crafts Quadrangle** - summer student at work in sculpture studio.

Fig. 78 **The Children's School** - shades of the Hall of Philosophy. Morning sessions are held for tots between 2½ and 6 years.

Fig. 79

Fig. 80

opposite page - top to bottom
Fig. 79 **Sherwood Studio** (1912) Palestine Ave. Named after William Sherwood, revered piano instructor: used for piano instruction.

Fig. 80 **The Lodge** (1912) - Chautauqua vernacular, originally an infirmary, now a staff residence hall.

Fig. 81 **Georges Barrere, flutist** - a bronze portrait sculpture executed at Chautauqua by Marian Sanford - in McKnight Hall.

Fig. 82 **"Piano Village"** - each of fifty-two diminutive practice studios is named after a well-known composer.

If we follow Palestine Ave. southward, in the direction of the Main Gate, we come upon **"Piano Village"** (Fig. 82) on our right - an unusual collection of diminutive, individual, practice studios. These are visual reminders of the hours of preparation preceding the many musical programs one enjoys while at Chautauqua. Enter **McKnight Hall** if for no other reason than to see the marvelous sculpture of renowned flutist, **Georges Barrere** (Fig. 81), executed by Marian Sanford in Chautauqua and cast in bronze in 1934. This is a wonderfully expressive piece of sculpture. The arc-roofed structure is a rehearsal studio; Fig. 83 illustrates Nathan Gottschalk, director of the excellent Chautauqua Festival Orchestra putting his charges through their paces prior to a performance in the Amphitheater. If we have commenced these perambulations sufficiently early, and it is not yet eleven o'clock, we might step over to the Main Gate to see what produce the **Farmer's Market** (Fig. 85) is offering on this day.

Fig. 83 **Director Nathan Gottschalk** rehearses the Festival Orchestra.

Statement by Nathan Gottschalk, Conductor, January 12, 1984 – Schenectady, N.Y.

Chautauqua has played an important part in my music career and I am grateful that it continues to do so. In a sense, my presence at Chautauqua since 1973 represents a second coming to that venerable Institution. I was a member of the Chautauqua Symphony Orchestra under Walter Stoessel and returned every summer until his passing. This also coincided with my entering the army. In 1973 I received an invitation to return to direct the Music School and develop the Festival Orchestra. I accepted the challenge enthusiastically. Since my return I have received enthusiastic support from two administrations which has enabled me to build and develop an outstanding Festival Orchestra of college age talents. This has been, and continues to be, most fulfilling and enriching for me. I would also like to feel that the lives of the students and the entire Chautauqua community have been likewise enriched. Chautauqua is not only music as everyone knows. Chautauqua has it all! a kind of Gestalt experience. It is living a life of values. How can it not be a meaningful experience? Each year I look forward to doing my part to make it better than last summer. I know of no place quite like it.

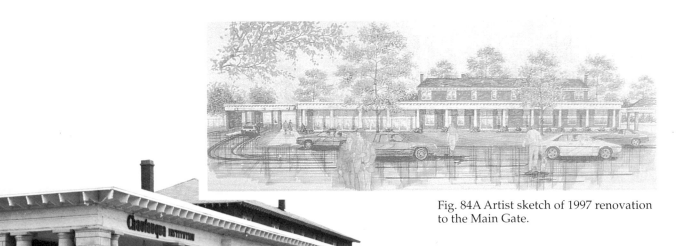

Fig. 84A Artist sketch of 1997 renovation to the Main Gate.

Fig. 84 **Main Gate to Chautauqua Institution** (1917) - originally an interurban stop on the Mayville to Jamestown line.

Fig. 85 **Farmer's Market** at the Main Gate - mornings from 9 to 11 AM.

Fig. 85A **Elizabeth S. Lenna Hall** on Palestine Avenue (1993) serves as a rehearsal facility for the Chautauqua Symphony Orchestral and the Music School Festival Orchestra.

Fig. 85B Interior of **Lenna Hall,** an 8,000 square foot, air conditioned and heated facility, configured for a chamber music recital.

The **Elizabeth S. Lenna Hall** was a gift to the institution from Reginald and Elizabeth Lenna of Jamestown, New York. Great emphasis was given by the architect, Robert Benchat of the Philadelphia firm Assembly Places International, to the best possible acoustics. The building may be "tuned" with retractable acoustical curtains located in the high "hat shaped" roof.

opposite page - top left
Fig. 87 **United Presbyterian House** veranda (1890) overlooks Palestine Ave. and the Amphitheatre.

opposite - top to bottom
Fig. 89 **Athenaeum Hotel** - the baroque stair was introduced in the course of extensive restorations in 1983. Its cast-iron, fountain center-piece was acquired from The Silver Dollar Trading Company of Colorado.

Fig. 88 **Patio** (newly developed) between the Amphitheatre and the Athenaeum Hotel (main north entrance visible). A place for quiet contemplation.

overleaf - page 70, top to bottom
Fig. 90 **Athenaeum Hotel** (1881) Essentially Second Empire style, "Victorianized" by its vast veranda overlooking Lake Chautauqua. (Baroque stair being installed - June, 1983.)

Fig. 91 **Athenaeum Hotel** - detail of its scroll-saw bracketing.

Fig. 86 "**Park Place**" makes a fine backdrop for the **Carnahan-Jackson Garden.** United Presbyterian House at left.

Next, let us stroll down Palestine Ave., past the **Carnahan-Jackson Memorial Garden** (Fig. 86) and the **United Presbyterian House** (1891) - the veranda of which is pictured in Fig. 87 - to the **Athenaeum Hotel** (Figs. 89-95) which was opened in 1881 only seven years after the founding of the Chautauqua Institution. It is a large building; the original reservation-board indicated 160 rooms. What an ambitious project so early in the life of Chautauqua. It is said to have been built in 90 days at an original cost of $125,000 with funds provided by founder Lewis Miller, his brother Jacob Miller and Clement Studebaker, successful carriage (then automobile) manufacturer. (Jacob Miller built, c 1880, one of the more flambouyant Victorian cottages at Chautauqua on the site now occupied by The Women's Club (Fig. 98) at 30 S. Lake Drive. A riot of open scroll work and spindles, it was torn down in 1929 to make way for its successor. The Studebaker "cottage" still exists at #39 North Lake Drive.) That the Athenaeum was among the very earliest buildings anywhere to be lighted by electricity may be attributed to Thomas A. Edison's connection with Chautauqua; he had installed electricity in his father-in-law's house (the Lewis Miller cottage) as early as 1879.

The principal entrance to the Athenaeum has traditionally been that which we are approaching at its north end (Fig. 88). From it, a corridor leads to the main hall and reservation desk. This hall, at right angles to the corridor, gives access to a spacious veranda, facing Lake Chautauqua, which extends from one end of the structure to the other - over

200'. It is flanked on the south by an attractive dining room with dimensions of 58' x 75', capable of seating three hundred persons, on the north by a very spacious lounge, 35' x 75', furnished entirely with old wicker. These rooms have trussed ceilings thereby doing away with the usual obstructive columns. Its advanced design was carried out by Mr. A.K. Warren, Superintendent of Grounds and Buildings. We would categorize its architecture as "American-Victorian Summer Hotel Style." However, it is interesting to note that if stripped of the grand veranda, with its 30' high posts and scroll—saw detailing, stylistically it would be fairly straightforward "Second Empire."

Fig. 89

Fig. 88

Fig. 90

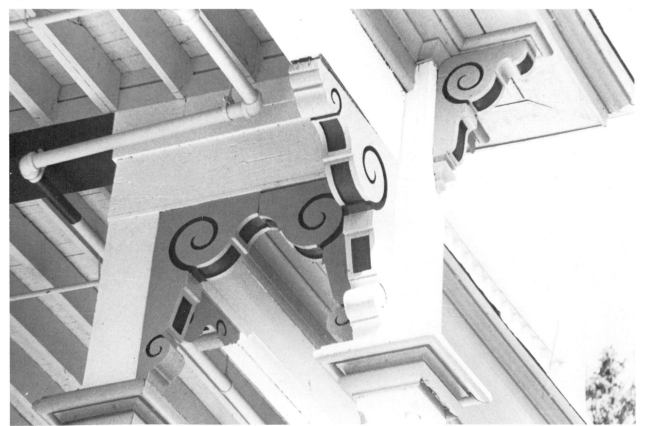

Fig. 91

70

Fig. 92 **Athenaeum Hotel grand parlor** - trussed ceiling construction did away with usual columnar supports both here and in dining room.

opposite page
Fig. 95 **Cast-iron fountain** installed in 1983 as a center-piece for the gracious dual stair-case on the Athenaeum's lake-side facade.

Fig. 93 **Athenaeum Hotel** - its veranda is sheltered by a roof supported by dozens of 30' high columns. Note the private balconies.

Fig. 94 **Athenaeum Hotel** - illustrating octagonal extension of the veranda; Arcade Building in the background.

Fig. 95

Originally, the 145' high, central, tower-pavilion contained an additional Mansard element, above that now existing, which included a spacious suite. This was removed at some point in time. An extensive restoration of the Athenaeum was undertaken, commencing in 1982, with monies from the Second Century Fund. Many of its decadent elements have been rebuilt, the principal public rooms refurbished, the porch extended with roomy, terminal polygonal elements at either end and the exterior repainted in an interesting combination of Victorian colors, to wit: parchment walls, pale rose column tops and accents, plum doors, sand window tops, white window door and columns, pine-needle green window sash. The structure cries for attention in its smashing, new, one-hundred-year overcoat! A major, aesthetically pleasing 1983 addition by architect Robert C. Gaede of Cleveland, in charge of the restoration, is the beautiful, curving, dual-stair providing access, from the porch, to the spacious grounds and the lake below. This has an its centerpiece a Victorian cast-iron fountain obtained, we are advised, from the Silver Dollar Trading Company of Colorado. The Athenaeum is, now once again, something to behold! The quote which follows is from a news release at the time it was completed in 1881:

> "There is no modern appointment lacking in this great structure. The first class barber shop, the telegraph office, the telephone office, electric bells, gas and electric lights, hot and cold baths, magnificent parlors, large rooms—well lighted and ventilated, elevators, music—everything to make it most complete. The table is such to tempt the appetite of a lods (?), the servants are attentive, the guests cultured, the proprietor genial and gentlemanly, and the terms moderate."

Wensley House (Fig. 96) is near the Athenaeum at the foot of Bowman Street. Now owned by the Institution, it provides attractive accommodations for speakers and performers visiting Chautauqua with affable Winnie Lewellen as hostess. News conferences with these celebrities are frequently held in late morning on its lovely porch overlooking Lake Chautau-

Fig. 96 **Wensley Guest House** (1881) Foot of Bowman Street. First a boarding house, converted in 1966 into a guest house for visiting lecturers and performers.

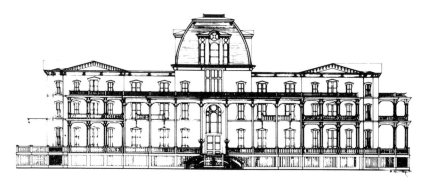

Fig. 97 **Athenaeum Hotel**

qua. Wensley House was built in the same year as the Athenaeum, namely 1881, as a rooming house earlier known as The Lafayette. It was acquired by Nina T. Wensley, wife of a Cleveland industrialist, in 1952 and given by her to the Institution in 1966 at which time the interior was remodelled. Mrs. Wensley was a member of Chautauqua's Board of Trustees for many years. Pres. Arthur Bestor lived here during his first three years at Chautauqua.

The reader may be impressed, as the author has been, by the loyalty and the philanthropy of the many persons for whom Chautauqua has been an important part of their lives. Consider, for a moment, Anna M. Kellogg's gift of Kellogg Hall, Mrs. O.W. Norton's gift of Norton Memorial Hall, Mrs. A.M. Smith's gift of Lincoln Dormitory, the Roblee Memorial Garden (behind Smith Library) and the Carnahan-Jackson Memorial Garden, the Ida Vanderbeck Chapel, and many endowed lecture series, etc. etc. etc. Chautauqua has the great quality of making dedicated friends!

While in this area there are a few other buildings which demand our attention. These, located along South Lake Drive between the Athenaeum and Janes Street, all face the lake and are fronted by spacious lawns. First we come to **The Woman's Club** (Fig. 98) at 30 S. Lake immediately identified by its gracious, tall-columned portico. Kidd and Kidd, architects from Buffalo designed it in the Neo-Colonial style. It was built in 1929, the year of the great stock market crash, on the former site of Jacob Miller's Victorian fantasy, as has been earlier noted. The spacious parlor, extending the width of the structure, is most attractively furnished with pieces in the American Empire, Victorian and Eastlake styles. There are suites upstairs. The Woman's Club is extremely active in sponsoring lectures and money-raising activities for the benefit of Chautauqua. The **Frances Willard House**, (one-time WCTU Headquarters) at #32 S. Lake Drive (Fig. 100), immediately south of The Woman's Club, is, from an architectural standpoint, one of the more interesting houses on the grounds. It is indeed an "eye-stopper." We would, considering its complex plan, steep roofs and irregular silhouette, categorize it as being in the "stick style" - a distinctly American innovation of the post Civil War, Victorian period. What a splendid complement it was to Jacob Miller's fantasia! The private dwelling was purchased by the WCTU in August of 1924 on the 50th anniversary of the organization's founding at Chautauqua in 1874. At that time a window - it must have been beautiful - was transferred from Anna M. Kellogg Hall, where WCTU offices had been located, to this new home. This window was subsequently moved to WCTU headquarters in Chicago when the house was acquired by the Haller family in 1946. Originally, the oblique, lateral gables had scroll-saw work complementing that in the front gable.

Fig. 98 **Chautauqua Women's Club** (1929) 30 S. Lake Ave. in the neo-classical style replaced the former, flambouyant, Victorian cottage of Jacob Miller, brother of founder Lewis Miller.

Retracing our steps northward along the Promenade before the Athenaeum, Wensley House and The William Baker Hotel, we take note of an additional Institution-owned building - **The Arcade** (Figs. 4, 101). This sizeable structure was erected at a cost of only $10,000 in 1891! Mr. E.G. Hall of Jamestown, New York, was the architect. Considering its multi-gabled construction with pent roofs, so similar to that at The Hall of Education, it is a reasonable assumption that this architect designed the latter was well. (We also know that the CLSC Alumni Hall came from his drawing-board). The Arcade has served many uses: doctor's offices were, at one time, housed on the second floor; earlier Sherwood Hall, named after piano instructor William H. Sherwood, seated 500 persons on the third floor; the ground floor seems always to have been reserved for shops including, prior to 1930, The Chautauqua Book Shop. Vernacular in style, with shingles stained pine-needle green, it forms an agreeable, architectural backdrop for the south boundary of Miller Park. As this is written it is said to be for sale. A venerable part of Chautauqua, listed on the National Register of Historical Buildings, it deserves careful watching.

Fig. 100 **The Frances Willard House** (c. 1883) 32 S. Lake Ave. A highly attractive, High-Victorian cottage employing a unique plan. WCTU headquarters from 1924 for two decades.

Palestine Park lies east of the Arcade Building between South Lake Drive and the Lake. Its north and south parameters are the children's beach and the shuffle board courts respectively - a distance of approximately one quarter mile. On a brief, earlier visitation of Chautauqua, I had stumbled across stony outcroppings labelled Jericho, Jerusalem, Bethlehem, etc. within this area - not knowing that I was in a place known as Palestine Park. These stony protrusions puzzled me, but I did not then dwell on their significance. Only upon my return to Chautauqua to record these impressions, when electing to take a Sunday evening tour of the Park, did I become fully aware of the fact that this was, indeed, an outdoor relief map of the Holy Land, to the scale 1-3/4 feet to the mile, with the land contoured to indicate the low-lying Dead Sea in the southeast, the Jordan River, Mr. Hermon in the north and many of the more important biblical towns west thereof. The shoreline of Lake Chautauqua actually resembles that of the Holy Land - albeit in reverse direction. The Park was laid out within a year or two of the establishment of the Assembly and rebuilt, pretty much as we see it today, in 1888. We must ever keep in mind that the work of Chautauqua in those early days was "normal training with the purpose of improving methods of biblical instruction in the Sunday School and the family" (the words are those of John Heyl Vincent). Children attending the boys and girls classes in those early years were taken on "pilgrimages" through the Park from time to time. It is an interesting aspect of Chautauqua to this day.

opposite page - top left
Fig. 99 **Willard-Haller Cottage** - detail of the gable scroll-saw work.

Fig. 101 **The Arcade Building** (1891) - attractive "back-drop" at south end of Miller Park - given to shops on the ground-floor, dormitory use above.

Fig. 102 **"Ashland House"** (1903) #10 Vincent

Miller Tower (Fig. 105) located nearby at what was originally known as "Fairpoint", was dedicated in 1911 as a memorial to founder Lewis Miller. Built largely of brick, rising to a height of 69 feet, it is supported by one hundred deep-driven piles. More or less in the form of an Italian campanile, its Italianate open gallery (Fig. 104) contains fourteen, good-sized McWeely bells at least one of which came from the demolished, Hi-Victorian **Pier Building** erected in 1886 on the site now occupied by the Youth Activities Center. Miller Tower has come to be the symbol of Chautauqua, as well as a landmark visible over great distances by the boating set. The land on which it stands is hallowed, in a sense, by the tens of thousands who for years disembarked at the nearby Pier Building - the principal portal to Chautauqua Institution into this century - where steamers arrived from Jamestown every hour. Imagine the steamer trunks which were unloaded and hauled up the hill to the Athenaeum, the St. Elmo, the William Baker and elsewhere.

Fig. 103 **Beeson Youth Center** (1968) headquarters of the boys and girls camp-clubs.

Fig. 104 **The Miller Bell Tower** - detail of its Italianate belfrey.

Fig. 105 **The Miller Bell Tower** (1911) erected as a memorial to Lewis Miller.

CHAUTAUQUA'S COTTAGES

We have now come to the point of considering the cottage architecture at Chautauqua. There are certain features that stand out. We have already noted the ubiquitous **front porch** - in boarding houses often stacked two, three and four high, one above the other, as dramatically illustrated by **The Spencer Hotel** (Fig. 108, 1907) located at the corner of Palestine and Wythe., also **The Ashland** (Fig. 102, 1903) located at #10 Vincent, and more modestly by The Chautauqua Inn (Fig. 106, 1876) at #16 North Terrace. The latter, painted white with brilliant yellow trim, built by a cobbler named Beaujeau, was originally known as The Beaujeau Boarding Cottage. Finally, we cite the picture-book **Bayberry House** (Fig. 14, 107) at #16 Simpson, also painted yellow with white trim. This is said to have been built c. 1881 for the WCTU. The prevalence of the front porch is the most conspicuous feature of Chautauqua's cottage architecture as well. The front porch, as an outdoor sitting room, as an extension of the interior living space to the out-of-doors, is a peculiarly American innovation in western architecture. It was espoused, as we have seen, by Andrew Jackson Downing whose **Architecture of Country Houses**, first published in 1850, was influential for decades in establishing American tastes in house design and decoration.

A second, prominent feature of cottage design at Chautauqua is the popularity of **board and batten construction.** This is a building system in which the weather boards are mounted vertically over the framing or studs with the cracks between them being sealed by milled strips known as battens. This system, too, was espoused by Downing who states on page 51 of the aforementioned book:

> "We greatly prefer the vertical to the horizontal boarding, not only because it is more durable, but because it has an expression of strength and truthfulness which the other has not. The main timbers which enter into the frame of a wooden house are vertical, and hence the vertical boarding properly signifies to the eye a wooden house."

The builders at Chautauqua certainly heeded this dictum; seldom, if ever, in my architectural travels have I encountered a greater incidence of board and batten construction which is frequently accompanied by widely overhanging eaves. The comparatively high incidence of this archaic building system adds greatly, too, to the uniqueness and the quaintness of Chautauqua.

The Smedley Cottage (Fig. 109, c. 1889) at #11 Morris Street, is illustrative of board and batten architecture at Chautauqua. William Larymore Smedley, its longtime occupant, was a painter of some note. Its ownership has since passed on to his daughter, Thaline Brewer, so that Smedley cottage has been in the same family throughout this century.

Fig. 106 **The Chautauqua Inn** (1876) #16 North Terrace Ave.

opposite page - bottom
Fig. 108 **The Spencer Hotel** (1907) corner Palestine and Wythe Aves.

One of Smedley's seascapes is displayed at the Smith Library. Mrs. Brewer owns many - amongst them an exceptionally beautiful portrait of her mother.

"Park Place" (Fig. 112), on the Brick Walk, immediately south of the Amphitheatre, makes a stunning back-drop for the Carnahan-Jackson Garden at the corner of Palestine and Clark - thanks to its board and batten construction.

The **Joseph Patton Cottage** (Fig. 110), #15 Whitfield, is said to have been at least partially built over a tent-platform in the 1870's. Earlier known as "Fairport Cottage," it is of some historical significance as having been the original office of **The Assembly Herald** - Chautauqua's first newspaper. Beyond its board and batten construction notice also, the quite lovely scroll-saw brackets. The cottage is painted in the popular combination of light yellow with white trim. The **Ritts-O'Reilly Cottage** (Fig. 181, c. 1881) at #14 Cookman, newly painted tan with rust trim under a moss green roof, is further illustrative of the B & B mode.

One seldom encounters board and batten construction today. Perhaps, with modern machinery, it is cheaper and faster to fashion clapboards (tapering thickness) than to tongue and groove the vertical weatherboards. Perhaps, despite Downing's protestation, the clapboard affords more positive weather protection. Also, perhaps today, and this is the most likely rationale, we prefer to accent the horizontal; verticality was desired in earlier carpenter-Gothic designs.

Fig. 107 **The Bayberry House** (c. 1881) #6 Simpson Ave.

Fig. 108 **The Spencer.**

Fig. 109 **Smedley-Brewer Cottage** (1880) #11 Morris Street

Fig. 110 **Joseph Patton (also "Fair Point") Cottage** (c. 1876) #5 Whitfield

A third, prominent feature which adds to the gaiety of Chautauqua's cottages is the fanciful **scroll-saw work** with which their verge-boards are frequently decorated. Verge-boards, or barge-boards, are placed on the verge or incline of a gable to screen the projecting roof timbers, and to prevent the penetration of rain. The medieval barge-board was morticed into a vertical post at the ridge of the roof called a "knop," (cf. Fig. 111, also Fig. 142) which gave a vertical accent at the roof peak. Furthermore, in the 1860's and '70's it became popular to externally extend the "collars," which tie-together and stabilize the rafters, beyond the wall surface to the barge-board and to join it with the knop, so that there was much "going on" at the peak of the gable (cf. Schwartz-Ebert-Burger cottage #17 Morris, Fig. 114). The invention earlier in the 19th century of the machine powered fret, or jig-saw, made scroll-saw work inexpensive and fun. There was great freedom in pattern design which the carpenter would simply trace or draw onto the barge-board, bracketing, finials, etc. If the boards were to be pierced, a hole would be drilled and the fret or jig-saw blade inserted therein; if the edge were to be irregular, the pattern would be traced and cut with a band-saw at a mill. This became an exuberant folk art! The presence of so much of it at Chautauqua adds immeasurably to its charm. This whimsical decoration is often popularly referred to as "Gingerbread" which the dictionary defines as "something showy, but unsubstantial and inartistic." We prefer to refer to it as "scroll-saw work" or "wood-lace."

In this respect, two cottages in particular at Chautauqua captivate the viewer for their cuteness and originality: the so-called **"Gingerbread Cottage"** (Fig. 11) at #34 James and the **"Peony Cottage"** at #22 Center Street (Fig. 173). The latter, built by J. C. Barkdull in 1879 (or 1895?) on a tent platform, is sheathed with wood siding. The lattice-work in the gable peak, filling the triangular spaces formed by the vertical knop and collar, is an entirely original treatment; likewise the dainty, open arches which make a 'triptych' of the porch. The planar balusters of the balcony rail above are cut so as to simulate a shape associated with turned stone and/or wood balusters. The cottage contains a living room across the front with a stair to one side which provides access to two bedrooms and a bath on the second floor. There is a diminutive dining-room and a kitchen behind the living room. The cottage was acquired by long-time Chautauquans Fred and Helen Theurer in 1969 and winterized. Mrs. Theurer, who passed away in 1977, was well known as a long-time director of CLSC and a devoted Chautauquan.

The **"Gingerbread Cottage,"** located at 34 Janes on the edge of Lincoln Park (gift of Mrs. John C. Lincoln and Mrs. Frank Newberry of Cleveland) was also built on a pre-existing tent platform. The construction date of 1891, mentioned in the literature, seems somewhat late in that the Carrier family of Rockport, New York are said to have owned it for five generations; also one might have expected conversion from tent to permanent dwelling at an earlier date. The main floor living-room retains the original old pine walls in

Fig. 111 **"Tionesta"** (1876) #12 Miller Park, - the Dithridge-Herman Cottage, like many others, was built on a tent platform.

Fig. 112 **"Park Place"** (1885?) Clark Ave. ("Brick Walk")

their natural state. Ms. Pauline Fancher, formerly librarian of the Smith Library, and author of **Chautauqua: Its Architecture and Its People**, is the fortunate, current owner. Chances favor her dating of it as being correct. The fretwork observed on the verge-board and bracketing, but particularly that within the balcony rail is delicate and highly attractive. The lovely pattern of the latter is also seen in the Follansbee Cottage (Fig. 133).

We would like, at this point, to single out several other neat cottages for special mention. This first of these is the **Alfred M. Landon Cottage** (Figs. 6, 116) facing Miller Park at the corner of Whitfield. Landon was, of course, the 1936 nominee of the Republican party who lost the subsequent election to Franklin D. Roosevelt. The Landon cottage was built by his grandfather, W. H. Mossman, in 1876 within a year or two of the founding of the Chautauqua Assembly. It is, therefore, one of the very oldest cottages on the grounds. Devoid of scroll-work, the things that make the Landon Cottage so special, aside from its historical interest are: quaintness of scale, attractive paint scheme - gray overall with pink trim - the delicacy of the porch and balcony balusters and its choice location overlooking Miller Park. Mrs. Ann MacMillan is the present owner.

Fig. 113 **The Lucases Cottage** (c. 1875) #5 Thompson Court (behind Miller Park row).

Fig. 114 **Schwartz-Elbert Burger Cottage** (c. 1879) - Board and Batten construction with collar, knop and mild, scroll-saw decoration.

The entire row of cottages facing Miller Park, of which the Landon Cottage is one, are all worthy of attention. That at #12 (Fig. 111), with the sign **"Tionesta"** hanging above its stoop, was also built in 1876 on a tent platform. It was for many years owned by Rachel Dithridge, a poetess, and is now enjoyed by her daughter, Mrs. Rachel Herman. The parlor, directly within the front door, is again lined with the narrow, vertical, tongue-and-groove pine boards which we have seen in Alumni Hall, in Normal Hall, in the "Gingerbread" Cottage and elsewhere. There is a bedroom to the left of the parlor and a dining room/kitchen at the rear. The gable, facing Miller Park, is one of the better examples of a knop morticed into a collar including decorative elements. Its yellow and white paint scheme is in nice contrast with the blue and white scheme of the **Wilder Cottage** (Fig. 115) next door at #8 Miller Park. The pierced treatment of the latter's gable, also the same symmetrical arrangement of doors and windows as seen at the "Gingerbread" Cottage, suggest that the same carpenter may have been at work. Its typically Chautauquan front porch, furnished in old wicker, is illustrated in Fig. 19.

Fig. 115 **Robert Wilder Cottage** - carpenter Gothic, painted light blue with white trim. One of Chautauqua's most charming!

Fig. 116 **Alfred Landon Cottage** - here the Presidential nominee spent summers with his grandfather, the Rev. W. H. Mossman.

The **Lucases Cottage** "Dixie" (Fig. 113), located at #5 Thompson Court, behind the cottages we have been considering, carries a dateboard claiming that it, too, was constructed circa 1875. These cottages, skirting the original Assembly Amphitheatre which was located in Miller Park, are among the very oldest at Chautauqua. "Dixie" is painted white with pink trim. One can be quite certain that the dormer and extension of the left wall outward, compromising its original symmetry, were later modifications. These understandable, but aesthetically unfortunate additions, coupled with the metal, deck rail replacement, are bothersome, but "Dixie" remains an "eye-stopper." Its superb location overlooks Lake Chautauqua.

#10 Morris Street (Fig. 117) is another of the attractive little cottages which would appear to have been originally built on a tent platform. Painted white with dark green trim, it occupies a very visible site at the head of Morris Street - one of Chautauqua's oldest - overlooking Bestor Square. Much better that it had been left in its natural state without the applied aluminum siding! One wonders what fret-work or wood-lace might have been removed in its 'modernization.' Notwithstanding, it is difficult to overlook this neat period-piece. In October, 1983 it appeared that this cottage would be "over-powered" by the new Glen Park condominium.

Fig. 118 **Porch** of the Farwell-Roehm-Panebianco cottage.

opposite page - top left
Fig. 117 **#10 Morris Street** - cute, most attractive
(in white with dark green trim) but compromised
by its aluminum siding.

We commenced these paragraphs discussing scroll-saw
decorative effects. While the **Farwell-Roehm-Panebianco** cottage (Fig. 119) at #21 Palestine Ave. has no present evidence
of such, it is well to point it out while considering some of
the more interesting 'petit' cottages on the grounds.
Overlooking the redeveloped plaza before the Amphitheatre,
it dates to 1878. Its vertically applied weatherboard is the
sole thickness of the walls so that its structural members are
exposed within. One enters a central stair-hall; sometime
before the cottage was purchased by the Panebiancos (1977)
a partition was removed from the parlor to its right (cf. Fig.
120) thereby forming one larger room where two had existed. The kitchen, directly behind, appears to have been a
shed-roofed addition of many years standing. There is a rental suite to the left of the center-hall where the partition has
been left in place. The Panebiancos occupy an upstairs suite.
Its quaint front porch (Fig. 118), furnished with old wicker
and a suspended, wooden swing, typical of Chautauqua,
prepares one for the charming interior furnished with the
Panebianco's antiques.

Fig. 119 **Farwell-Roehm-Panebianco Cottage,**
(1878) #21 Palestine. Its walls are one board thick.

Fig. 120 **Farwell-Roehm-Panebianco Cottage** - the
parlor is furnished with the Panebianco antiques.

Fig. 121 **Bestor Plaza** viewed from the Colonnade Building's second floor administrative offices.

Fig. 122 "**Little White House**" (c. 1870) #17 Roberts - one of the more attractive cottages at Chautauqua by any measure. **Edgewood Apartments** at right.

Color Plate - facing page
Top left - **Chautauqua Post Office** (1909), Bestor Plaza - Book Store entrance at left.
Top right - **Welch's Pavilion**, Fountain 'house' - southeast corner of Bestor Plaza.
Bottom left - **Morning lecture** at the Amphitheatre.
Bottom right - **The Chautauqua Inn** (c. 1876) 16 North Terrace Ave.

Moving on to some larger cottages exhibiting an exuberance of scroll-saw work, let us first focus on #17 Roberts (corner of Miller), sometimes referred to as the "**Little White House**" (Fig. 122), owned until the early 1980's by Jeanette Robbins. In a conspicuous location, it is readily seen when standing before Smith Library or the sheltered font at the SE corner of Bestor Plaza. The delicate "wood-lace" bracketing, both upstairs and down, seems almost to form a series of arches on both levels. Its decorated facade is topped by the attractive fret-work in the single, under-scaled, totally decorative gable. Slim, attenuated porch columns assist in imparting a quality of daintiness to the whole. The **Edgewood Apartments** to its right, dating to c. 1885, further illustrate multi-decked porches ubiquitously observed at Chautauqua. Consider how stark either of these facades would be without their veranda.

Fig. 123 **Golden Arch** below the Hall of Philosophy through which CLSC candidates pass on Recognition Day.

With its newly applied polychromatic paint scheme, there is no cottage on the grounds more arresting than the **Baird-Wineman Cottage** (Fig. 127) at the foot of Peck Avenue (#5). The vergeboards, together with the perforated brackets and panels framing the porch bays, are in a soft salmon shade; the lattice work in the gable and the railings are in cream; the horizontal member at the base of the gable as well as the latter's soffit are in a rust, earth-tone. The major wall surfaces of the house itself are painted cream while the trim is salmon. Notice that the front entrance is canted at a corner of the facade. This is not an uncommon feature of cottage architecture at Chautauqua about which we will have more to say. The Baird-Wineman house bears a date-sign indicating that it was built in 1874 - the year Chautauqua was founded. This seems very early for so elaborate a dwelling; perhaps the date refers to there having been a tent-platform in place at that time. Files in Smith Library indicate its date of construction as c. 1895; this, in turn, seems a bit late for such flambouyant decoration. Earlier owned by a Mrs. John B. Humble of Buffalo, N.Y., the house was acquired by the Baird-Wineman families in 1962.

Fig. 124 **Denise-Hagerman Cottage** - detail of the scroll-saw work.

Let us now turn our attention to the **Denise-Hagerman Cottage** at #10 Bliss Street (Fig. 126). Bliss, which extends obliquely from the NE rear corner of The Colonnade Building, is another of the older streets at Chautauqua. The site for this cottage was leased for a tent in 1876. The present cottage was built, at least partially, over a tent-platform in 1896. It was purchased by Rev. Larimore C. Denise in 1910 and is now owned by his daughter, Mrs. Dorothy Hagerman. Thus, like the Smedley Cottage and others, it has been in the same family for virtually three-quarters of a century. The fret-work in the gable, the delicacy of the upstairs porch balusters, together with the quaint treatment of the porch door, are the features particularly deserving of our attention. Note also that the exposed ends of the rafters, at the eaves, exhibit scroll-saw work - a unique feature. The parlor is directly within the front door which was purchased from an 1896 Sears-Roebuck catalogue. A stair to the right provides access to the second floor bedrooms. A combination dining room/family room, behind the parlor, extends the width of the cottage. This precedes a kitchen and a wood-shed at the left rear corner converted to cupboard space. The front porch, at some point in time, was doubled in size by the Rev. Denise. (The **Edward Shields Cottage** (Fig. 128) immediately next door, at #12 Bliss, is where the author resided while registering these impressions.)

The **Nelms-Beeson Cottage** (Fig. 129) at #25 South Street, which looks out upon the green before Alumni Hall, has a gable and upstairs porch, door treatment which is the mirror image of that at #10 Bliss. It was certainly built by the same carpenter and, no doubt, at about the same time, viz. 1896 - 97. The Beeson Cottage, as it appears today in our photo,

Fig. 125 **Ernst Walker Cottage,** #21 Peck Street, is highly visible from the Brick Walk.

opposite page
Fig. 127 **The Baird-Wineman Cottage** (late 1870's) #5 Peck Street. A riot of color in addition to the scroll-saw work make this charming cottage an eye opener. cf. color plate #6 page 107.

represents the joining of two building units approximately 50 years ago, according to Mrs. Beeson - one from a still empty lot down the hill on South St. having been joined to the original with the decorated gable. Mr. Beeson's family gave the **Youth Center** (Fig. 103) at the foot of Park St. as a memorial to their parents.

The **Ernst Walker Cottage** at #21 Peck Street (Fig. 125) immediately behind Lutheran House is most attractive. One can hardly miss seeing it when traversing the Brick Walk en route to the Hall of Philosophy;—its double-decked porch extends outward bekoning for attention. This unusual, oblique extension of the porch, combined with its delicate, incised bracketing and the ever-present, colorful bouquet of cut-flowers framed by the upstairs porch posts, make it picture-book pretty. Here again we observe a canted front entrance. Consider how much the wood-lace brackets would be missed if, by chance, removed at the suggestion of a well-intentioned painter, as sometimes happens.

Fig. 126 **The Denise-Hagerman Cottage** (1896) #10 Bliss Street, red with white trim, - an exuberant example of scroll-saw, folk art.

Fig. 128 **Edward Shields Cottage**, #12 Bliss - used by the author in the course of doing **Chautauqua Impressions.**

Fig. 129 **Nelms-Beeson Cottage** (c. 1896) #25 South Street - most certainly built by the same carpenter as #10 Bliss.

"La Chaumiere" (Fig. 130) at #6 Warren Street, overlooking Louisa Lincoln Park, adds its bit to the Chautauqua scene. Chaumiere, as if you did not know it, is French for a "quaint cottage" - this one built in 1887. No small part of "La Chaumiere's" attraction is its paint scheme - the cottage is basically mustard color with cream trim. The writer was somewhat surprised to observe, when examining the photos closely, that the gable fret-work (Fig. 130A) was carried out on a single piece of board - perhaps even tempered Masonite. This suggests that it might be a later-day replacement. No matter, it, and the bracketing below, are a folk art very much in the spirit of Chautauqua.

Fig. 131 **Dennis Beeson Cottage** - similarity in design to the Denise-Hagerman cottage is clearly visible.

Fig. 130A "La Chaumiere" - Fret-saw work in the gable, original or not, adds immeasurably to the viewer's delight.

Fig. 130 "La Chaumiere" (1887) #6 Warren Ave. Its color scheme is no small part of its attraction - mustard with cream trim.

opposite page
Fig. 133 **Follansbee Cottage** (c. 1882) corner Foster and Fletcher Sts. - most convincing specimen in the "stick style" at Chautauqua.

Walter McIntosh Cottage (Fig. 132) formerly the Rose Apartments, located at #12 Bowman, corner of Pratt Ave., enjoys a marvelous situation overlooking the busy plaza before the Amphitheatre. Fig.   was taken from its balcony to capture this fine prospect. The cottage grabs your attention for several reasons: first, perhaps, for the expanse of white railing, on two levels, with pierced balusters; next for the distinctive aqua-green color with which the wall surfaces are painted; then, for the dainty bracketing and slender posts, and finally, for the potted fuschias suspended between all posts in season. The McIntosh's, residents of far-away Brisbane, Australia (note the Australian flag), purchased the cottage in the early 1980's and have extensively restored it (the wood railings replace pedestrian ones of iron which they "inherited.") A major feature of the restoration was the conversion of three upstairs apartments into one cheerful, spacious family suite. The cottage was built c. 1882. Note the uniquely curved rose trellis in front (replanted) from which Rose Apartments derived its name.

Consider, now, the **Follansbee Cottage** (Fig. 133) at the corner of Foster and Fletcher Streets - a splendid example of the "stick style" very much in the mode at the time it was built c. 1882. What an expanse of porch! - screened-in upstairs. Note the collar morticed into a knop at the top of the steep gable; also the board and batten construction and the canted front entrance. We have seen the same porch rail at the "Gingerbread" Cottage (Fig. 11). Was it, perhaps, available from mills by the yard? The seven or more generations of Follanbee's who have come to Chautauqua have contributed importantly to its programs and its history.

Fig. 132 **Rose (or McIntosh) Cottage** (1882) #12 Bowman corner or Pratt. Here again, color draws our attention (aqua-green with white trim), also the prominent corner location.

Fig. 133 **Follansbee Cottage**

opposite page - top to bottom

Fig. 135 "**Box Seat**" - the Schaffee Cottage - corner Palestine and Clark Sts. - also "stick style" - so named because its porches overlook the Amphitheatre.

Fig. 136 **Shakespeare Cottage** - #20 Vincent Street - along with the fret-work note the hanging swing and rocker.

"**Box Seat**" (Fig. 135) the Schaffee cottage, on the Brick Walk at the corner of Clark and Palestine, is another convincing specimen in the "stick style." Like the McIntosh Cottage (Fig. 132) it is painted a distinctive green with white trim. Its name stems from the fact that, from its balcony, one can see and hear virtually everything that transpires in the Amphitheatre. The cottage was built in 1888. Behind, and to one side of "Box Seat," we see the columns of the Disciples of Christ House past which Chautauquans so frequently walk en route to the Hall of Philosophy. Our photo well illustrates the mature 'forest' in which Chautauqua is located. The abundance of trees adds immeasurably to the intimacy of the place and, of course, minimizes the need for air-conditioning.

Now observe the **Russell Schall Cottage** (Fig. 134) across the way at #20 Palestine for which we have a date of 1893. Aside from its expansive porches, bracketing and nicely turned balusters, the interesting feature of this cottage is the unique, second-floor oriel window at right. Note that, as with so many of the cottages we have viewed, the porch posts rather than being square and bulky, are turned to a slender, highly aesthetic dimension. Perhaps you have also noted that windows of the period tended to be tall and slender - no "picture" windows.

The most interesting feature of the **Shakespeare Cottage** (Fig. 136), at #20 Vincent Street, is the fret-work in the otherwise non-functional gable atop the porch roof. However, if you will look closely, you will observe that the dark-colored course (actually it is barn red) at the porch eaves is perforated with a hex motif. The porch is furnished, Chautauqua fashion, with a rocker and a suspended, slat-back, oak swing.

Fig. 134 **Russell Schall Cottage** (1893) #20 Palestine - oriel window, at right, and the wrap-around porch are the unique points of interest here.

Fig. 135

Fig. 136

DIFFERENT OR DISTINGUISHED

Fig. 137 **Fireplace** in hall (parlor) of the Whaley cottage; room is 20' x 30' with 18' ceiling.

In the preceding paragraphs we have focused on Chautauqua's ubiquitous verandas, the high incidence of board and batten construction and the decorative effects achieved with the scroll-saw. We have become aware of the wide range of paint colors employed on the body of its cottages as well as for trim. We have noted the not uncommon occurrence of the canted front door. Rarely, if ever, would one encounter this feature in contemporary American home building. It serves to remind us that at the turn of the century it was not uncommon to have canted or bevelled house corners, particularly at the second floor level. These provided the occupant with a wider range of vision than would have been possible if the windows were flush on a strictly rectangular facade. The reader will have observed that the cottages at Chautauqua were invariably fabricated of wood. Wood was plentiful; the skills to work it were at hand and it suited the environment. To this point, with only a few exceptions, the cottage architecture which we have considered has been in a vernacular style which is to say that it is "native and peculiar to popular taste" of the time. Some of it would pass for what is popularly called "steam-boat" or "carpenter" Gothic. The exceptions are the Follansbee and Francis Willard cottages and "Box Seat," each of which is in a distinctive American style - the "stick style." The Lewis Miller cottage, less convincingly, is also in the "stick style" which, together with the "shingle style" is generally considered to be one of the truly original architectural styles to surface in America during the 19th century. (Much else was a revival of some pre-existing style.) Buildings in the style generally tend to be tall with steep roofs and an irregular silhouette; diagonal "stick work" is very characteristic.

One should ever keep in mind while "house-watching" at Chautauqua, that this was, and still is, very largely a summer, vacation community. He ought not, therefore, expect to find the more sophisticated and pretentious residences that were then being built on Buffalo's Delaware Ave. or Cleveland's Euclid Ave. Until recent years comparatively few were winterized for year-around habitation. The intimacy resulting from 700 dwellings existing in close proximity over only 358 wooded acres (with brick walkways and controlled vehicular traffic) is another vital element in the pleasure of experiencing Chautauqua.

Let us now turn our attention to some larger and/or unusual cottages which make up the fabric of Chautauqua. At **#8 Simpson Street** (Figs. 137-140) there is a Classic Revival building with "Patrons of Husbandry" inscribed on its frieze. One might, with good reason, apply the term 'Greek Revival' to it except that the Greek Revival in America had largely spent itself by the mid-1850's. Stylistically, it is an anachronism. The shallow, roof-slope is Greek as dictated by the Parthenon; the broad frieze board is from the Greek vocabulary. The Doric columns, albeit

Fig. 138 **Fred Whaley Jr. Cottage** (1903) #8 Simpson - former Grange headquarters beautifully adapted to summer residential use.

Fig. 139 **Stained-glass window** in kitchen (left rear corner) of Whaley Cottage.

Fig. 140 **Whaley Cottage** - charming garden-patio at its rear.

without entasis, make direct contact with the stylobate (in this case the porch floor) without benefit of a base in true Doric fashion. #8 Simpson Street might as well - ought to have been - built in 1850 rather than in 1903. The Grange, original owners of this 'cottage' was founded in nearby Fredonia in 1868. Its building, in 1903, was funded by Cyrus Jones of Jamestown as a memorial to his father. 'Grange Day' was celebrated here on the 3rd of August for many years until, finally, it was purchased by Edwin D. Smith and converted into a dwelling. It was again purchased comparatively recently by Mr. and Mrs. Fred Whaley Jr. of Buffalo, New York, who have beautifully redecorated and restored it. One grand room opens to the visitor - once inside the front door - revealing a great fireplace eight feet or more in height with a frieze bearing triglyphs. Its dimensions are 20' x 30' with an 18' ceiling. This was the Grange meeting room. A doorway to its left rear gives entre to a 'picture-book' kitchen containing a marvelous, colorful, contemporary stained-glass window (Fig 139, it was criminal to photograph it in black & white). Its inconography is interesting; note an image of the 'cottage' in the lower left corner, above it representation of the Athenaeum Hotel - and to the right of the Hotel an image of the Bell Tower, to the right of the Tower a sailboat and in the lower right hand corner musical instruments - the Whaley's are musicians. A whale (for Whaley) can be made out above the sailboat; a weathervane atop the pediment is in the form of a whale. All told - a great adaptive use! (Fig. 141) is an oblique view from the rear.

The **Richard Maddy Cottage** (Fig. 143) at #21 Wythe, in the vicinity of Norton Hall, is different stylistically from any other dwelling at Chautauqua. Built c. 1905, it resembles a southern plantation house of the ante-bellum period with its wrap-around verandas on two levels. It mimics the Old South's variant of the Greek Revival which virtually became a national style in the interim 1830 to 1855. By the farthest stretch of the imagination, its plan suggests a small cathedral with nave and lateral transcepts abutted by the open gallery. Note that the "transcept" gabled ends have "returns" - a feature drawn from the Greek Revival vocabulary. The cottage is painted cream with white trim while the veranda ceiling contrasts in a sky-blue shade. One enters directly into a cozy parlor having an attractive fireplace on the inside wall; the dining room is beyond to the right, while the kitchen is at the left. Situated on a walkway, in a considerable open space for Chautauqua, one enjoys a fine arboreal vista from the verandas. This cottage, too, is an interesting variant amidst the architectural scene at Chautauqua.

Fig. 141 **Whaley Cottage** viewed from S. Terrace Street - perfect Greek Revival proportions.

Fig. 142 **Knop and collar** - morticing of the two members illustrated in an unidentified Chautauqua cottage.

Fig. 145 **United Methodist Missionary Home** (1888)
#34 S. Lake Dr. - originally the residence of Anna
Studebaker Carlisle whose father (coach-builder)
was a leading Chautauqua benefactor. Splendid
Arts and Crafts interior.

Color Plate - page 107
Top left - **Baird-Wineman Cottage** (c. 1895), #5
Peck Avenue - a riot of color!
Top right - **"Box Seat"** (1888), 30 Clark Avenue
at Palestine.
Bottom - **The Walter McIntosh Cottage** (1883), #12
Bowman Avenue.

The **United Methodist Missionary Home** (Fig. 145) located
at 34 South Lake Drive—obvious in its prime location on
the lakefront, also for its not inconsiderable mass and barn-
red color with contrasting white trim—is of particular interest for its stunning interior. Once inside, one is in a world
of the Arts and Crafts movement - a turning-away from Victorian frills in favor of hand-crafted, utilitarian design which
was coming into vogue when this cottage was built in 1903.
It was, indeed, originally the summer residence of Mrs. Anna Carlisle, daughter of Clement Studebaker, wagon-builder
who, as mentioned earlier, was a major contributor of funds
to the re-construction of the Amphitheatre along with the
Miller brothers. (He served briefly as president of the Institution in 1899 following the death of Lewis Miller.) The
Methodists acquired the structure in 1918 from Mr. Harry
Truesdale, a Chautauqua trustee. Back to the interior: the
parlor occupies the space to the right of the front door while
the dining-room is to the left. The hand-crafted woodwork,
the hearth ensemble, the lighting fixtures, the marvelous
Mission oak furnishings, are altogether as exciting an expression of the arts and crafts, in situ, as the author has ever encountered. These rooms are of museum quality.

Founder John Heyl Vincent's cottage, located immediately
south of the Missionary Home, burned to the ground in
1901. **The Bishop's Garden,** (Fig. 18) a memorial to him,
now occupies the site. Its center-piece is a circular pool
presided over by a nude, little boy with outstretched arms
sculpted by Ruth Sherwood, daughter of Prof. William H.
Sherwood of Chicago who, for years headed Chautauqua's
piano department. **St. Francis and the Wolf of Gubbio** (Fig.
146), a more impressive piece by Miss Sherwood, may be
seen along the Brick Walk before the east facade of The Hall
of Missions. In this St. Francis is shown with a bible in hand
- a wolf on its haunches at his left and, at his right, a
beautiful fawn. (The original casting of this piece occupies a
prominent position in San Francisco; reproductions are in
various U.S. cities).

The **Hukill-Lacey Cottage** (Fig. 148) across Peck Street at
#38 South Lake Drive, appears on an 1880 map of Chautau-
qua. However, its modified exterior, originally swathed with
fanciful Victorian fret-work, would not be recognizable to
contemporaries of that time. Its scroll-work and wood-lace
were completely removed in 1901. One wonders if the con-
flagration at the Bishop's cottage that very year might have
precipitated this drastic modification. The cottage's multi-
gabled Mansard roof was almost completely obscured by
foliage when our photograph was taken. It has been in the
Hukill family for generations since its acquisition by them in
1887 - sharing the choice lakefront location with several
distinguished-looking neighbors.

Fig. 143 **Richard Maddy Cottage** (c. 1905) #21 Wythe Ave. - unique stylistically at Chautauqua, it begs comparison with Greek Revival, plantation houses of the deep south.

Fig. 144 **Arboretum** - bordering Longfellow Avenue is maintained by the Bird, Tree and Garden Club.

Fig. 146 **St. Francis and the Wolf of Gubbio** - a
bronze sculpture by Ruth Sherwood, daughter of
piano instructor William Sherwood, located beside
The Hall of Missions.

Fig. 147

The McKec-Karslake Cottage (Fig. 150) at #44 S. Lake Drive, constructed c. 1896, is one of those neighbors. Observe that its two-story, wrap-around verandas are recessed under the roof - most are appendages. It is most unusual, to say the least, to see Adamesque swag designs, together with fluted, Ionic columns, on a Chautauqua cottage. These refinements are said to have resulted from concurrent Grecian travels by the original builder. Further expressions of these travels are seen in the three, impressive, interior fireplaces - each with mantel supported by turned, free-standing Ionic columns in different woods - framing attractive tile insets. The Karslakes have owned the cottage since 1950.

The former "President's House" (Fig. 149) at #1 Root Street is contemporary with the Karslake Cottage, both having been built circa 1896. During Arthur Bestor's long and eventful presidency many notable visitors to Chautauqua were received here including Franklin D. Roosevelt, Amelia Earhart and Admiral Richard Byrd - both the latter in July of 1929. Its silhouette is hardly tall enough or sufficiently intricate to be categorized as "Queen Anne", however, the

opposite page
Fig. 147 **Ida M. Vanderbeck Chapel** (1963) - a facility funded and maintained by the King's Sons and Daughters.

Fig. 148 **Hukill-Lacey Cottage** (c. 1880) 38 S. Lake Ave. - has been in the Hukill family for generations. At the turn of the century it was stripped of much delightful, flambouyant scroll-saw work.

opposite page - top to bottom
Fig. 151 **Children** join in the Recognition Day parade.

Fig. 150 **McKee-Karslake Cottage** (c. 1896) 44 S. Lake Dr. - Adamesque swags combined with several elegant, neo-classical, interior fireplaces are of particular interest here.

round tower with conical cap, is characteristic of the style. A large, picture window to the rear of the living room affords, a view of Lake Chautauqua. The house was remodelled and winterized in 1962 for Pres. Curtis W. Haug and family, however, during Oscar Remick's presidency (1971 - 77) 1501 North Lake Drive became the president's house. #1 Root Street is now owned by Richard Miller, the great grandson of founder Lewis Miller and a trustee of Chautauqua Institution.

Packard Manor (Fig. 154), said to have been inspired by Winston Churchill's "Chartwell," was built in 1916 on six and one-half acres adjacent to Chautauqua's northern boundary by William Doud Packard. His architects were, it is alleged, the prestigious New York firm of Warren & Wetmore who, among other important commissions, were designers of Grand Central Terminal (1903 - 13). William Doud Packard and his brother, J.W. Packard were the founders, in 1890, of The Packard Electric Co. at Warren, Ohio (they sold the firm circa. 1932 to General Motors). The author, when he first laid eyes on the house, knowing that Packard came from Warren, O., and observing the Jacobean Revival style in which it is built, harbored the strong hunch that architect Frank B. Meade of Cleveland was its designer.

Fig. 149 **Richard Miller Cottage** (c. 1896) #1 Root Street. For years, until 1970, the summer home of Chautauqua's presidents.

Meade designed in this style and was active in Warren at the time. Mr. Packard, who was virtually deaf, had a great fear of perishing in a fire; therefore he had the manor constructed so as to be as fireproof as humanly possible. Its walls are of solid concrete; its floors are one and one-half feet in thickness supported by 18″ steel girders. Its exterior brick is said to have been imported from England and the roof slate, each of which weighs thirty-six pounds, from Belgium. During the presidency of Curtiss Haug, Packard Manor was used by the Institution for entertainment and receptions, including among others, one for Indian Ambassador B. K. Nehru. Since 1957 the residence has been owned by Dr. and Mrs. Carl S. Winters - former staff lecturer at General Motors Corp. Mr. Packard, incidentally, lived in it for only three years.

Within, a commodious vestibule opens to a spacious center-hall flanked, on the right, by a large living-room beyond which there is a well fenestrated, brick-walled enclosure - a former solarium - which now serves as Dr. Winter's study. The dining-room is located at the rear to the left of the central hall. There is a large porch across the rear facade overlooking Lake Chautauqua. The principal rooms contain beautiful Adamesque cornices which have been painstakingly restored by Dr. Winters. The manor contains twelve bedrooms and eight baths on the second floor.

Fig. 151

Fig. 150

111

Fig. 154 **Packard Manor** (1917) North Lake Drive. Built, in the Jacobean style, by one of the Packard brothers of Warren, O. like the Rock of Gibraltar to be totally fire resistant. Owned, for a time, by the Institution, it has witnessed many receptions.

Fig. 155 **North Shore Condos** (1982 et sequitor) - a new, contemporary lifestyle being introduced to Chautauqua.

Fig. 153 **Meiers Cottage** (c. 1955) North Lake Drive - comfortable contemporary home fronting on Lake Chautauqua.

Fig. 152 **Meiers Cottage** - detail, front lawn slopes to the Lake.

Packard Manor is the only residence in the vicinity of Chautauqua with such grand pretentions and in so formal a style. An organ, originally installed in Packard Manor, was moved to The Hall of Christ at the time of Dr. Winter's purchase of the mansion from the Institution in 1957.

North Shore Condos (Fig. 155), a contemporary housing development, now occupies land which was formerly part of the Packard estate. In the summer of 1983 units were selling for as little as $75,000. The **Meier Cottage** (Fig. 153), adjacent to Packard Manor at the northern extremity of North Lake Drive, was designed in 1955 by Oliver Johnson, resident, apprentice architect on the Packard job. It enjoys a fine prospect of Lake Chautauqua.

Fig. 154

Fig. 155

113

MORE COTTAGES

The **Compton - Freytag Cottage** (Fig. 157) located at the northeast corner of Pratt and Hurst, is one of my favorite dwellings on the grounds. The unique oriental character of the roof has much to do with this predilection; other factors are its commanding location combined with its attractive paint scheme of pale yellow with white trim. The cottage was built in the time-frame 1914 - 16. Its front door opens directly into a living room, furnished in a manner which complements the roof style, with a fireplace at the far end; behind this there is an eat-in kitchen. The right hand portion of the cottage contains two bedrooms separated by a bath. Mr. and Mrs. Charles Freytag, comparatively recent purchasers, rotate between this darling cottage and a Florida winter home.

The **Munger-Conway Cottage** (Fig. 156), located at #8 - #10 Hurst, was constructed in 1918 in the then popular bungaloid style. Its builder combined fieldstone with brown-stained shingle to achieve a most attractive effect. Today, a breezeway joins what must originally have been two or more living units. These were deeded to Chautauqua Institution in 1954 and used to house music students. The Conway family of Shaker Heights, O., purchased them in 1980.

Fig. 156 **Munger-Conway Cottage** (1918) 8 - 10 Hurst Street - bungaloid style. For a time, from 1954, used as a music school dormitory.

Fig. 157

Fig. 158

115

Fig. 160 **Jones-Copeland Cottage**, #20 Whittier - a "British Colonial" design at Chautauqua.

The **Gail Berg Cottage** (Fig. 158), at 19 Hurst Street across from Freytag's, is exemplary of what can be done with contemporary design at Chautauqua. Constructed of western, rough-cut cedar, stained a light gray, it blends well with its neighbors and the natural environment. It has porches at either end (the one not revealed in our photo is more spacious) and a sun deck at the rear. Examined critically, its silhouette is not that much different from board and batton cottages built 100 years previously.

The **Luder Cottage** (Fig. 159), located at the lower end of Park Ave., is another contemporary model which fits well into the Chautauqua environment. It is not surprising that when the Luder's decided to build in 1976, they retained architect Eugene Swartz of their home-town, Chillicothe, Ohio as their designer. The living room has a cathedral ceiling which may be dramatically viewed from an upstairs balcony-bridge leading to the bedrooms.

Author Anthony Adamson in his excellent book, **The Gaiety of Gables: Ontario's Architectural Folk Art**, refers to an architectural style which he terms 'British Colonial' - a one and one-half story block surrounded on two or more sides with a veranda. Structures of this type appeared at colonial military posts about the empire, e.g. that at Fort Niagara, Ont. **The Jones-Copeland Cottage** (Fig. 160) at #20

Fig. 159 **The Luder Cottage** (1976) 6 Park Ave. - perhaps Chautauqua's earliest contemporary cottage.

Whittier (extreme south end of the grounds) in the one structure at Chautauqua which could be said to be in this style. One wonders if its builders might have been British Colonials. Subsequently, in speaking with the Copelands, we learned that the Joneses patterned the house after a small villa seen in Italy. To us it more closely resembles Adamson's 'British Colonial'. Notwithstanding, the cottage is most attractive enhanced by the oil painting which its current owners display to the right of the front door.

The **Genevieve Cheney Cottage** at #18 Cookman Street (Fig. 162, 1899) faces the Hall of Philosophy and cannot - ought not - be overlooked in considering the cottage architecture at Chautauqua. Its distinguishing feature is the delightful third floor balcony recessed within dual, intersecting gables in a most unique manner. This feature is illustrated further in Fig. 163 photographed from the steps of the Hall of Philosophy. It, together with neighboring porches, makes a fine, grand-stand seat from which to hear proceedings in the Hall. The body of the house, constructed in 1899, is sheathed with clapboard; the intersecting gables have a shingle covering installed in an unusual, circular swirl pattern. The cottage to its left in our photo, #20 Cookman, makes an interesting foil in which a pitched roof uniquely intersects a gambrel roof at a right angle. Aesthetically, they make a synergistic combination.

Fig. 161 **Genevieve Cheney Cottage** - aspect from the southeast in autumn reveals yet another porch recessed within a gable.

Fig. 160

Fig. 162

Fig. 163

Fig. #164 illustrates two interesting cottages, #37 and #39 Janes, fronting on Lincoln Park. #39 at the right, known both by the names **'The John Deere Cottage'** or the **Keating Cottage**, defies stylistic categorization. Following evening performances at the Amphitheatre, while traversing Lincoln Park, one looks for the brilliantly illuminated goose displayed high up in its gable window. #37, to its left, another of the many board and batten cottages at Chautauqua, groans under its burden of added dormers, but is none-the-less an attractive part of the Chautauqua scene. It was, for years occupied by Mrs. G. R. Alden, an author known as "Pansy", after which the cottage takes its name. The Keating Cottage was built in the time-frame 1885 - 90; its neighbor most certainly preceded it.

Who could pass The **Mustard Seed Cottage** (Fig. 168) at #47 Root, corner of Palestine, without a hesitation in his gait? The cottage, appropriately painted mustard color, was built in 1919. Note how it endeavors to emulate older and larger cottages on the grounds with the touch of scroll-saw work applied to its dual windows. What a cute retreat from which to partake of all that Chautauqua offers!

With so many architectural variants who would be surprised that there is a log cabin at Chautauqua? The **Charles**

opposite page - top to bottom
Fig. 162 **Genevieve Cheney Cottage** (1899) #18 Cookman (right) - vernacular, interesting, well-maintained, it overlooks the Hall of Philosophy.

Fig. 163 **Cheney Cottage** - detail taken from the Hall of Philosophy.

Fig. 164 **Keating Cottage** (c. 1898) #39 Janes (right) and neighbor at #37 Janes (left)

Fig. 165 **#26 Center** - a true bungalow.

Fig. 166 **Charles A. Ferguson Cabin** (1880's) 16 Peck Ave. - Chautauqua's one and only.

A. Ferguson cabin (Fig. 166) dates to the early 1880's. It has wide-plank flooring fastened with hand-made nails, a hearth and chimney of native field-stone and maybe even a latch-and-string door closure. Observe the wicker wash stand, the wicker rocker, the hanging porch swing and the American flag. On the early morning when we photographed the cabin a late model Cadillac with Florida license was parked in the driveway. Could it be that the inhabitants of this Daniel Boone-ish shelter drive a Cadillac and pass the balance of the year in a plush Boca Raton condo?

The **Brown Cottage** (Fig. 167) at #5 Roberts, built in 1895, is deceivingly cute (Webster - "pleasing, pretty or dainty.") Packed into it there is a living room, a dining room, a kitchen and three bedrooms. Its outer skin is brown-stained shingle. Our photo illustrates what a camera can do in isolating something from its surrounding - not that its surroundings are all that bad, but that they do dwarf this charming bungalo-ette.

There are not many true bungalows at Chautauqua. Maxine M. Carleton's at **#26 Center Street** caught our eye. Marcus Whiffen in his **American Architecture Since 1780** has this to say about the Bungaloid style:

"The true bungalow is a small single story house; the roof-space may be made liveable by a single dormer or by windows in the gables, but anything approaching a full second story disqualifies the building for the title bungalow. The adjective "bungaloid" is applicable to the numerous houses that do their best to look like bungalows while having a second story—houses "built along bungalow lines" as they were called."

Fig. 167 **The Brown Cottage** (1895) #5 Roberts Ave.

Fig. 168 **The Mustard Seed Cottage** (1919) #47 Root Ave.

Fig. 169 **H. M. Bailey Cottage** - Cook Street

The Crockett High House (Fig. 170, opposite page) at 20 South Terrace is typical "old Chautauqua" - if anything at Chautauqua could be said to be typical. It enjoys a fine prospect, from its perch, down Miller Street, overlooking what formerly was the Grange (Fig. 103), to the lake. Milton Twitchell built the cottage in 1903; the Ralph Crocketts acquired it in 1974.

By Whiffen's definition, the **Bailey Cottage** (Fig. 169, 1905) which stands alone on Cook Street beyond the Arts and Crafts Center, is not then a "true bungalow" - there is too much 'going-on' upstairs. Henry Turner Bailey, father-in-law of Helen M. Bailey who owns this cozy cottage was, as has been previously mentioned, the designer of the nearby Art Center; also an early director of same. Helen Bailey, operator of the first Art and Craft Shop in the Colonnade Building, has been associated with Chautauqua for at least 60 years during which she has hardly ever missed a summer session. Son-in-law, architect Robert C. Gaede, was commissioned, in the early 1980's, to do the restoration of The Athenaeum Hotel and is the designer of its stunning, new, lakefront, dual stairway. The Bailey cottage's dining room is to the immediate left of the entrance - a stair to the second floor to its right; the living room extends across the rear of the cottage. There are three bedrooms and a bath upstairs. Architect Gaede has appended a small, ground-floor room for his personal use during fleeting visits to Chautauqua visible at the right in the accompanying photo.

Fig. 169A **The Campen House,** 34 Miller Street, (c. 1881) was constructed on what had originally been a tent platform.

Fig. 170 **Crockett High House** (1903) 20 S. Terrace Ave. – high it is!

Fig. 171 **Bernice Group Cottage** (1879) #14 Bliss Street

"**Camelot Cottage**" (Fig. 172). This well-preserved specimen of board and batten construction commands one's attention at the corner of Vincent and Wythe. Its occupants can move about the wrap-around porch, furnished with the usual rockers and ceiling-suspended swing, to catch the sun or to avoid it, as suits their whim.

Fig. 172 **Camelot Cottage** (1883 est.) #22 Vincent Ave. - another highly attractive board and batten cottage.

Color Plate - facing page
Top left - **The Miller Bell Tower** (1911) - symbol of Chautauqua.
Top right - "**The Aldine**" apartments, Bowman Avenue at Simpson.
Bottom - **The Compton-Freytag Cottage** (1914-16), corner of Pratt and Hurst. An oriental touch.

Fig. 173 **The Fred Theurer Cottage** (1879), at #22 Center Avenue - another of Chautauqua's more delightful carpenter Gothic cottages.

#26 **Cookman St.** (Fig. 174), at the corner of Clark, is one of the few cottages at Chautauqua which could truly be called "Queen Anne" style; it has the prerequisite bay windows, multiple roofs meeting at right angles, polygonal turret, and large porch gable. According to library records, it was built in 1900. At one time, we are told, it served as headquarters for the Unitarians at Chautauqua. One has only to walk out upon its quaint upstairs porch to hear and survey all that goes on in the Hall of Philosophy directly across the way.

The Miller Cottage (Fig. 180), constructed in 1899, is located on a perch at #30 Wythe immediately north of Norton Hall. Sheathed with brown shingles, its lines are accentuated by white trim. Note the unusually wide overhang of its south gable; also that most windows are glazed with multiple, square panes. It is vernacular - yet different from other cottages of its time which we have considered herein.

The Dr. Mary Noss Cottage (Fig. 182) at #5 Merrill St., below the Hall of Philosophy, was built in 1883, or so the sign to the right of its front door proclaims. The interesting features here are the "wall dormer" and prominent corner posts, the design of which is echoed in the porch posts.

Fig. 174 **W. Phillip McConnell Cottage** (1900) 26 Cookman Ave. at Clark overlooking The Hall of Philosophy was, prior to 1972, Unitarian headquarters at Chautauqua.

Fig. 175 **W. Phillip McConnell Cottage** detail #26 Cookman Ave.

The **Forest B. Irwin Cottage** (Fig. 176 c. 1887) at 39 Palestine was built just within Chautauqua's north boundary only a dozen years following the founding of the Assembly. From the misalignment of the upstairs porch rails and the divergent treatment of the lower porch - not to mention the discordant hip-roof dormer - it is a reasonable assumption that the left hand portion of the cottage was a later addition. Painted yellow with white trim, the cottage is not one easily passed by. Since 1955 it has been owned by the Irwins; Mrs. Irwin (Alfreda) was a longtime editor of the **Chautauquan Daily** and authored the popular **Three Taps of the Gavel.**

D'Amato-Forest Cottage (Fig. 178) at 47 Hurst was constructed in 1927. Its style, unique at Chautauqua, brings to mind the work of the English architect, C.F.A. Voysey for its expansive, cream-colored, rough cast wall surfaces and steeply sloped gables.

Jones-Dunbar Cottage (Fig. 177, 1907) 39 Cookman Avenue. This non-descript, but interesting, vernacular cottage caught the author's eye many times, but there was always an auto parked before it to mar a potential photograph - until autumn. There is something of the Texas ranch house in its design and, indeed, W. Goodrich Jones, its builder came from Temple, Texas. Note the tree, as old as the house itself, growing through the porch floor and roof.

opposite page - top to bottom
Fig. 176 **The Forest B. Irwin Cottage** (c. 1887) #39 Palestine Ave.

Fig. 177 **The Jones-Dunbar Cottage** (1907) #39 Cookman Ave.

Fig. 178 **D'Amato-Forest Cottage** (1927) 47 Hurst Avenue.

Fig. 179 **Florence Pettit Cottage** (1911) 34 Scott Ave.

Fig. 180 **Miller Cottage** #30 Wythe Ave.

Fig. 181 **Ritts-Fowkes Cottage** (1878) #14 Cookman Ave. - board and batten, tan with rust trim and moss green roof.

Fig. 182 **Dr. Mary Noss Cottage** (1883) #5 Merrill Ave.

Fig. 183 **Artist Revington Arthur** conducting a demonstration at The Arts and Crafts Center.

Fig. 184 **O. Gilbert Burgeson**, naturalist, briefing a group before a Saturday morning nature walk.

Fig. 185 **Three Summer Rusticators** pass time on Bestor Plaza.

overleaf - top to bottom
Fig. 187 **Flea Market** - held annually in July behind the Colonnade Building.

Fig. 188 **CLSC Headquarters** - impromptu readings take place each Friday noon.

far overleaf - top to bottom
Fig. 189 **Battery Operated Trams** were a 1983 people mover innovation.

Fig. 190 **Recognition Day Parade** - the one day in the year when CLSC banners are brought out into the light-of-day.

Activities Album

Fig. 186 **Arts and Crafts Sale** before the Post Office on Bestor Plaza - a frequent Friday diversion.

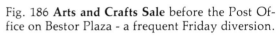

Fig. 187

Fig. 188

Fig. 189

Fig. 190

Fig. 191

Fig. 192

Fig. 193

Fig. 194

Fig. 195 **The Beechover**, a guest-house, flies the flag for its final season. It is scheduled for demolition to make way for a condominium. The combination of a roof-top cupola with a Mansard roof is rather curious.

AUTUMNAL EPILOGUE

We returned to Chautauqua, mid-week in mid-October, to further consult files in Smith Library, to refresh our memory of a few interiors (none of which were open) and to take additional photos of Chautauqua garbed in autumnal earth tones. From Erie we elected to take less-traveled, scenic Route 430 through Finley Lake and Sherman. The foliage, in its coloration, was considerably more advanced than along Lake Erie's shore - no doubt due to the higher elevation. Chautauqua's Gate House was wide open - no guards, no cards to show. Absorbing the scene, that I had now been living for months, we slowly proceeded via Ramble and Vincent, past Bestor Plaza to Miller Park. The sky was ominous, there was a stiff wind, we had never before seen the Lake so angry. Since rain was predicted, it seemed wise to do some photography without delay.

It was a different Chautauqua than that which we had left in August. Streets which had throbbed with life were now, except for a comparatively few tradesmen and carpenters, all but deserted. They were "topping-off" the new Glen Park Condominum facing Bestor Plaza at the head of Morris Ave. (the reader may recall that its foundation laid open during the previous summer), re-roofing the Women's Club and erecting a new cottage at #19 S. Terrace, corner of Miller. Ground-keepers were busily winterizing the Bishop's Garden fountain center-piece. Its "boy-figure" by sculptress Ruth Sherman had been removed to more secure winter quarters as had also, we noted, her "Saint Francis" beside Mission Hall. Most buildings were locked-up; all but a few cottages closed and secured for the winter - porch furniture, hanging planters and window boxes removed for its duration.

Fallen leaves congregated in street gutters while others danced in the strong, autumn wind. Those which momentarily clung to their branches were, we felt, at very nearly the peak of their autumnal color. Chautauqua was serenely beautiful, but it was empty, deserted - a later day Pompeii, for a measured time. All but a very few, die-hard winter residents had packed-up and departed to resume their lives in small towns and bustling cities across the country, or to a Florida winter retreat. At eight in the morning one could walk, as I did, from the Colonnade Building to the Hall of Philosophy without encountering another soul. Miller Bell Tower's carillon was silent. The limited supply of donuts at the seasonally 'jumping', but now quiet Colonnade grocery would, we were told, be quickly snatched-up by the tradesmen for their morning coffee-break. The home-made bread table was bare, but bread could be special ordered for next day delivery.

Aside from the Administrative offices where personnel were, not doubt, assessing the past season and planning for the next, Smith Library was the major focus of life in this largely deserted, Victorian community. Post season, the library opens at 9:30 AM and commences to close at 4:30 PM. The paucity of readers and book-borrowers, we observed, made for enhanced comraderie amongst the personnel who have Thursdays off as a cost-cutting measure. The Book Store, too, was open - its staff greatly reduced - and not now busied by the early morning traffic for the **Daily Chautauquan.**

Leaves were accumulating in the open, empty Amphitheatre where throngs congregated little more than six weeks earlier; what a spring clean-up job, we reflected. Winter at Chautauqua, we were told, is rough for most; only strong persons with great inner resources stay on. But those who remain find winter a great time for reading, for contemplation, for renewal - and for anticipation of the next summer Assembly.

Fig. 196 **"Little White House"** (c. 1870) #17 Roberts - one of the more attractive cottages at Chautauqua by any measure.

BIBLIOGRAPHY

Chautauqua: Its Architecture and Its People (1978)
by Pauline Fancher
Banyan Books, Inc. Miami, Florida

Chautauqua Publications (Concise Historical Sketches) 1934
Arthur Eugene Bestor Jr.
Chautauqua Press

**Chautauqua: A Center for Education, Religion and Artists
in America** by Theodore Morrison (1974)
University of Chicago Press

Three Taps of the Gavel (1977 Reprint)
Alfreda L. Irwin

The Gaiety of Gables: Ontario's Architectural Folk Art (1974)
Anthony Adamson and John Willard
McClelland & Stewart Ltd. Toronto

**The Architecture of Country Houses: Design for Cottages,
Farm Houses and Villas** by Andrew Jackson Downing (1850)
Dover Reprint

Villas and Cottages: A series of Designs (1857)
by Calvert Vaux
Da Capo Reprint 1968

Modern Architectural Designs and Details
Amos J. Bicknell & William Comstock (New York, 1881)

Architecture in Fredonia (1811 - 1972): Sources, Context
Development by Daniel Reiff (catalogue to exhibition)
State University of New York, Fredonia

19th Century Houses of Western New York (1966)
by Jewel Helen Conover
The State University of New York Press

The Shingle Style and the Stick Style (1971 Revised)
by Vincent J. Scully Jr.
Yale University Press

The Chautauqua Movement (1886)
by John Heyl Vincent
Chautauqua Press

American Architecture Since 1780
A Guide to the Styles
by Marcus Whiffen M.I.T. Press

Fig. 197 **Baird-Wineman Cottage**, 5 Peck Avenue, exemplifies the exuberance and the gaiety of the carpenter Gothic mode.

Statement by O. Gilbert Burgeson, Naturalist

Being a naturalist and a conservationist, I am very impressed with the beautiful 'architecture of nature' found in and about the Chautauqua Institution. The stately trees found throughout the grounds are matched in very few places. The gardens, in front of homes, contain specimens of ferns and shrubs that one would expect to find only in virgin forests. On one recent nature walk we identified fifteen species of ferns and twenty of trees. My interest in Chautauqua dates back sixty-five years when first married. My wife's grandfather was one of the first Methodist preachers attending the Sunday School Assembly the last two weeks of August each year at Fair Point, as Chautauqua was then called; they all lived in tents.

I have followed the growth of Chautauqua Institution ever since and am very proud of the part it has played in providing culture, education and entertainment to peoples the world over. I am glad that in my humble way that I have had a part in promoting nature study that is now part of the total Chautauqua experience. (Cf. Photo at bottom of page 132)

O. Gilbert Burgeson
December 20, 1983
North Palm Beach, Florida

Author's note: Mr. Burgeson is a gentle and kindly man whose stature has grown in his selfless dedication to service.

INDEX
(Figures in bold face type indicate photographs)